EQUIPPING FOR KINGDOM HARVEST

FOUNDATIONS IN *Evangelism*

Darlene Cothron
— FOREWORD BY JOHN ECKHARDT —

Printed in the United States of America. All rights reserved under International Copyright Law. This book or parts thereof may not be reproduced in any form, stored in a retrieval system or transmitted in any form by any means – electronic, mechanical, photocopy, recording, or otherwise – without the express written permission of the author or the publisher.

Unless otherwise indicated, all scripture quotations, references and definitions are from the Authorized King James Version © 1987; The New King James Version © 1982 by Thomas Nelson, Inc.; The New International Version 1973, 1978, 1984 by International Bible Society by the Zondervan Corporation; The Amplified Bible Old Testament © 1962, 1964, 1965, 1987 by the Zondervan Corporation; The Amplified New Testament © 1954, 1958, 1987 by the Lockman Foundation; The Message. Copyright © 1993, 1994, 1995, 1996, 2000, 2001, 2002. Used by permission of NavPress Publishing Group. All rights reserved; M.G. Easton M.A., D.D., Illustrated Bible Dictionary, Third Edition, published by Thomas Nelson, 1897; The Name Book © 1982, 1997 by Dorothy Astoria. Bethany House Publishers; The Discerning Christian: How the Believer Detects Truth from Error in the Midst of Today's Religious Confusion © 1990 by Dr. Kenneth Neil Foster. Christian Publications, Inc.; United States of America, Social Security Administration resource for historical information on welfare and assistance for the poor www.ssa.gov/history/pdf/histdev.pdf.

FOUNDATIONS IN EVANGELISM:
Equipping for Kingdom Harvest

Darlene Cothron
NowKingdomCulture@gmail.com

Copyright © 2013 Darlene Cothron
ISBN # 978-0-9890892-1-0

Published by Heavenly Enterprises
773.783.2981 • Chicago, Illinois

FOREWORD
JOHN ECKHARDT

It is an honor to do the foreword to this book on the subject of evangelism by Darlene Cothron. I have seen Darlene's passion for evangelism over the years. Her desire to see people come to salvation through the gospel has been passionate and consistent for many years. I was impressed with the depth of this manuscript, and the careful articulation of the subject. It is an in-depth and well done book that will add to the discussion of evangelism and discipleship.

Darlene comes out of an apostolic community of believers and understands the importance of prayer and the Holy Spirit in evangelism. This book reveals the many aspects of successful evangelism that includes divine encounters and opportunities orchestrated by God. Evangelism is not accidental, but the plan and purpose of heaven. Evangelism can and should be an exciting journey of faith that results in great testimonies of God's grace and power.

I would recommend this book as a training manual for leaders who desire to equip their members for outreach. It will be an invaluable tool in raising the level of evangelism in a local assembly. It would be great for every believer to be taught a systematic course in evangelism. Evangelism is a key to church growth and the advancement of the kingdom.

Darlene's desire is more than personal, but apostolic as well. In other words, she desires to see the church mobilized and SENT OUT in evangelism. She has been a part of training believers to be a part of advancing the Kingdom of God for many years. She understands that evangelists and evangelism must be a part of the church if it is to be truly apostolic.

I have ministered throughout the world, and I am still amazed at how little evangelism is emphasized in many churches. This important subject has to be taught over and over to keep the church mindful of what is important to God: SOULS. The church is often so INWARD until many have ceased being OUTWARD.

This book is not only about evangelism, but practical ways of reaching the lost. This book provides strategies for effective outreach. We can talk about evangelism all day, but not PRACTICE IT. Evangelism is more than a good teaching, it is an action. We must be doers of the Word, and not hearers only. Once our minds are renewed, our actions will follow. Remember the early church is first seen in the book of ACTS.

I believe in the power of impartation. I believe that grace can be imparted from one believer to another. I believe you can receive impartation through preaching, teaching, laying on of hands, and even through books. What Darlene has can be imparted through her words. Receive a greater anointing for evangelism as you read the words of this book.

Darlene points out that "evangelism is a lifestyle." It should be a part of every believer's life. It must be taught from the pulpit. Evangelism is not just for evangelists, but it is for all believers. Believers must be challenged and provoked to become evangelistic.

Foundations in Evangelism - Equipping for Kingdom Harvest

This book goes beyond evangelism, and discusses discipleship. It is not enough to win the lost, but they must be taught. This is the key to multiplication. The more people are saved, taught, and released back into the harvest, the more the kingdom advances.

We desperately need greater wisdom and understanding in the area of evangelism and discipleship. As you consider what is written in this book, I believe the Lord will give you a greater understanding of evangelism. Those already active and successful in evangelism will be refreshed. Those who have lost their zeal will be recharged. Those who have been discouraged will be encouraged. Read this book prayerfully, and allow its contents to bless you as you move forward and be a part of bringing in the harvest.

John Eckhardt
December 2012

Foundations in Evangelism - Equipping for Kingdom Harvest

ACKNOWLEDGEMENTS

To all my brothers and sisters who have assisted me along the way, many of whom are a part of the Crusaders Church family. Thank you for encouraging me to start this project and see it to completion. I especially would like to acknowledge the evangelism department members who have challenged me, prayed for me, and been incredibly supportive in so many ways over the course of this book project and in ministry overall. May God multiply blessings unto you all.

I would like to thank my special covenant sisters and fellow ministers in the faith, Tonya Roberson and Christy Minger for being such great role models not only in the evangelism ministry but in life as faithful women of God. You both met me when I was just ten months old in the Lord and through your demonstration of love and commitment I learned the value of discipleship and now enjoy the blessing of you both being as family to me. Pamela Huggins, my special covenant sister who is also as family to me and met me in my first four months of salvation, you challenged me to be a witness during that first year and pushed in getting me to my first CIA New Orleans Outreach in 1988. You didn't know you started something back then and you continue to cheer me on today. Thank you for your love and support.

I extend a special thank you to my pastor, Apostle John Eckhardt, who has supported me in this project and released powerful and revelatory teaching for more than two decades that has blessed my life; your teachings have set the paradigm for my work in ministry. To Prophet Wanda Eckhardt, who has supported the work of the ministry at Crusaders since the very early years. You have nurtured and given to so many, and continually challenged me to get this book done, a special thanks to you for your support.

I extend my heartfelt thanks to my loving and supportive parents, Otis and Charlie Mae Cothron (Mom went home to be with the Lord), who were there for me from the start. Mom you were my inspiration, great encourager and best friend. I miss you dearly. Daddy, thank you for continuing to carry the family torch and the sacrifices you made all my life. You demonstrated faithfulness year after year throughout my childhood and it is a character trait that I value today. My grandparents whose love knew no end, for all your support through my early years, college years, and my entire life, I thank you and miss you. God used you to invest much into my life.

Denny and Sandy Nissley and the Christ In Action (CIA) family, as I sat under your umbrella of wisdom and training, you brought another level of faith into my life that challenged me to be bold for Christ and sacrificially committed to the work of evangelism. Thank you for your example and showing so many the love of Christ In Action.

I would like to thank the talented group of God's servants that sacrificed and devoted administrative time to design a book cover image, edit, print and bind the original draft book that preceded this book as a gift to me (Marie Hobson, Timothy and Monica Lacey, Catrina Harris, Christy Minger, Davina Wilson) you all are awesome. I value your love and continued commitment.

To the editors that utilized your years of experience and invested hours of labor to help me in this project, words cannot express my appreciation for your guidance, wisdom and encouragement.

Marilyn Alexander at Heavenly Enterprises, you literally pursued me in your emails, text messages, calls and encouragement to get this book completed. You are a jewel. Thank you so very much.

Most importantly, to my God and Lord Jesus Christ, who pursued me in His love many years ago. You have forgiven me of sin and called me Your own and have anointed me and given me such a great privilege to serve You and be an ambassador of the Kingdom. Lord, You have kept me and blessed me through this journey of faith, I am so very grateful. Thank you Lord!

Foundations in Evangelism - Equipping for Kingdom Harvest

TABLE OF CONTENTS

Foreword .... John Eckhardt

Preface ....

SECTION I
A Passionate Love For Jesus
    Love And Compassion For The Lost 1

The Apostolic Mandate
    The Role Of The Believer 12

Personal Evangelism
    Introducing People To Jesus 21

Sharing A Personal Testimony 36

Cell Ministry
    Evangelism And Discipleship 44

SECTION II
Make Disciples Of All Nations 59

Compassion Ministry
    The Father's Love Through Demonstration 80

Strategic Prayer And Evangelism 92

Evangelistic Strategies For Kingdom Harvest 115

Culmination 136

PREFACE

This book is a combined series of lessons written as a part of the course work for the evangelism training provided to those who have desired to embrace the call to evangelism. The lessons have been organized and placed in book format to be used as a training tool for others. The desired goal is that many believers would be encouraged, challenged and ignited with passion for effective and strategic evangelism that will yield multiplication of disciples. Each chapter focuses on a particular aspect of evangelistic ministry while providing foundational teaching. Chapters one through three are to be read in continuum while each of the remaining chapters have been written to stand alone as a complete lesson. Although the reader may choose a particular title of interest to study from chapters four through nine, it is recommended that all the chapters be read in order. The questions that are provided at the end of each chapter allow for individual review of chapter content and reflection.

The first lesson in chapter one provides an opportunity for the reader to do a personal assessment of their spiritual journey and love for Jesus Christ. It emphasizes the importance of having a right motivation for evangelism that proceeds from a passionate love for Jesus and compassion for the unsaved. The alternative would be performance based evangelism that is done out of spiritual obligation and works, which is not the desire of God for His people.

Many believers give reasons such as lack of training, motivation, fear and many other reasons for not committing to the work of evangelism, yet God has commissioned all His spiritual sons and daughters to be a witness for Him. This book addresses the obstacles to the work of evangelism while challenging the reader to overcome these obstacles in the strength and power of the Holy Spirit.

Although practical guidelines and methodology in evangelism ministry are addressed within the book, the importance of the role of the Holy Spirit as the lead partner in ministry, along with strategic prayer, are emphasized. The strategies reviewed in this book are given to provide insight into being more deliberate and effective in evangelistic efforts. God has unlimited strategies to release unto His people in the work of evangelism that are relevant for each season, culture and generation.

There have been many books written on the topic of evangelism and many more will be written in time. My prayer is that this book will become a useful tool for individual believers and ministries to further the work of evangelism and discipleship in order for a greater Kingdom harvest to be realized in our present time.

SECTION I

Foundations in Evangelism –
Equipping for Kingdom Harvest

Foundations in Evangelism - Equipping for Kingdom Harvest

-ONE-
A PASSIONATE LOVE FOR JESUS
LOVE AND COMPASSION FOR THE LOST

FOUNDATION

Man was created for God's pleasure, yet sin separated man from God (Revelation 4:11). Because of Adam's sin and disobedience, judgment came upon all men and all were made sinners (Romans 5:18-19). All the earth had a sin problem for which no amount of sacrifices or burnt offerings could remedy (Hebrews 10:4). There was a need for a complete solution to the problem. The solution, ordained from the foundation of the world, came through Jesus Christ (Revelation 13:8).

> *Hebrews 10:14, For through one eternal offering, Jesus, the Lamb of God without spot or blemish, all who received Him were freed from the bondage of sin.*

What caused God the Father to respond to man's desperate need? What caused the creator of all things seen and unseen to extend so much mercy and compassion to those He created? Certainly the answer to this question is "LOVE." The Bible tells us, "For God so loved the world, that He gave His only begotten Son, that whosoever believeth in Him should not perish, but have everlasting life," John 3:16. God's love for the world was so great that it caused Him to ACT and respond to man's desperate need for deliverance.

Today many still remain in bondage to sin not knowing or understanding God's plan of redemption, nor the penalty of sin. Many are unaware that they stand guilty before God because of their sin, while others are seeking freedom from sin and guilt through false religions and other ineffective methods. God desires that the world know the truth of His word and His plan of salvation. God has ordained that the church proclaim the truth of His word so that those that hear the gospel would call upon His name and be saved.

> *Romans 10:13-15, "For whosoever shall call upon the name of the Lord shall be saved. How then shall they call on Him in whom they have not believed? and how shall they believe in Him of whom they have not heard? and how shall they hear without a preacher? And how shall they preach, except they be sent? as it is written, How beautiful are the feet of them that preach the gospel of peace, and bring glad tidings of good things!"*

God commissioned the church to preach the gospel and teach all nations to observe His word (Matthew 28:18-19). Thousands of years since the commission was given, the mandate to preach the gospel to the entire world remains unrealized as there are people in the world today who have not heard the gospel message even once. Few, relative to the large numbers of professed Christians, have obeyed the commission and responded to the call of God as reflected by research statistics and simple observation. Why are the numbers so few when the need is so great? What will cause the church at large to obey the mandate and reach the world with the gospel? What will cause God's people to ACT and reach out to the world with a heart of compassion? Certainly the answer to this question is "LOVE." A passionate love for Jesus, born out of an intimate relationship with the Lord, will birth a love and compassion for the world and cause the church to ACT in greater numbers and fulfill the commission (John 21:15-17, I John 3:16-17). The heart of the church must be aligned with the heart of their heavenly Father and then the evidence of that alignment will be seen through obedience and action.

THE NEW TESTAMENT COMMANDMENT
Mark 12:30, "And thou shalt love the Lord thy God with all thy heart, and with all thy soul, and with all thy mind, and with all thy strength: this is the first commandment."

The first commandment in the New Testament commands us to love the Lord with all of our heart, soul, mind and strength. Not only are we commanded to love God, but to love Him with our ALL. This would mean loving God with everything we possess and nothing held back. Would we truly fulfill this first commandment by loving God any less than what He requires? The answer to that question is "no."

LOVE IN ORDER
Every professed Christian that is a true disciple of Christ, if asked who or what they loved, could probably provide a long list. The list would most likely include a love for God, spouse, children, extended family, friends, church family, etc. The list may also contain a love for a particular hobby, career, travel, food and a host of other things. If asked to prioritize the list, or to put people or items into categories, most Christians would probably list God as their first love either because it is a living reality or because the expectation is that God should be at the top of their list. Those who have shown evidence of a love for God in their lives through their lifestyle, time, commitment and overall Christian service would probably say "Yes, my love for God is at the top of

my priority list."

If one would do an assessment to evaluate the true reality of such a statement based on the daily lifestyle of the believer, what would be the result? Let's take a look at the church in Ephesus in the book of Revelation.

> *Revelation 2:1-5, "Unto the angel of the church of Ephesus write; These things saith He that holdeth the seven stars in His right hand, who walketh in the midst of the seven golden candlesticks; I know thy works, and thy labour, and thy patience, and how thou canst not bear them which are evil: and thou hast tried them which say they are apostles, and are not, and hast found them liars: And hast borne, and hast patience, and for my name's sake hast laboured, and hast not fainted. Nevertheless I have somewhat against thee, because thou hast left thy first love. Remember therefore from whence thou art fallen, and repent, and do the first works; or else I will come unto thee quickly, and will remove thy candlestick out of his place, except thou repent."*

It is very clear from the preceding passages of scripture that the church in Ephesus had done many things that were right and pleasing to God. They labored, had patience, did not bear evil, identified false apostles, and did not faint in the process. This sounds like the characteristics of true Christians that love God, and it certainly is. Nevertheless God brought something to their attention. They had left their *first love*. Even though they did many things that were pleasing to Him, the order of love within their hearts had somehow become out of order. God, over the course of time, had become second to something else in their hearts. It was clear that this particular church loved God, but He was no longer their *first love*. God commanded the church to repent of this sin. Not only were they commanded to return to their first love, but were commanded to do the first works. The scripture does not clearly show us what those first works were, but even the works we do for God today should be in the order or priority that He has intended.

Let us take the time to reflect on that moment in our lives when we first encountered Jesus and cultivated a *first love* kind of relationship with Him. What were our *first works*? Did those first works include telling others about Jesus Christ our Savior?

There are many who profess that they are Christians but have never truly had a life changing encounter with Jesus. Some have the experience of religious ritual or practices without an encounter and relationship with Christ. Those that have had that kind of life changing encounter, and have been truly born again, may be able to recount a desire to tell others about their newfound commitment and joy found in Christ. There was a desire to be a witness for Jesus and of His love so that all would experience such an encounter. What happened to the excitement and desire to tell others about Jesus? Is it still there?

A Change Of Heart

If, at any time, we as Christians find that our love for God is out of order, not fervent, or that we lack the zeal or passion that we once had, we must repent and seek the Lord. The church of Ephesus in the second chapter of the book of Revelation was called to repent when God was no longer their first love and we are called to do the same. God's desire is to renew us again and again, to revive us, and cause us to be fervent for Him that we not be "lukewarm" in our love for Him. Revelation 3:15-16 says, "I know your works, that you are neither cold nor hot. I could wish you were cold or hot. So then, because you are lukewarm, and neither cold nor hot, I will vomit you out of My mouth" (New King James Version). For many these scriptures may sound harsh, but through the word of God we come to understand our Lord's disdain for a church that lacks fervency as these words were first delivered to the Laodicean church. Yet because of His love, God brings correction and challenges His people to repent.

> *Revelation 3:19, "As many as I love, I rebuke and chasten: be zealous therefore, and repent."*

A change of heart begins with acknowledging that there is a need for change followed by repentance. True repentance involves godly sorrow and a broken and contrite spirit. The yielding of the heart and the will to God then results in a change of heart and mind through Holy Spirit transformation. After God supernaturally transforms us from within by His Spirit, the result of that change is seen in our obedient response to His word and His will. God dwells with those that are of a contrite and humble spirit.

> *Psalms 51:17, "The sacrifices of God are a broken spirit: a broken and a contrite heart, O God, thou wilt not despise."*

> *Isaiah 57:15, "For thus saith the high and lofty One that inhabiteth eternity, whose name is Holy; I dwell in the high and holy place, with him also that is of a contrite and humble spirit, to revive the spirit of the humble, and to revive the heart of the contrite ones."*

A HUNGRY HEART
What does it mean to "hunger" for something? One

definition for the word "hunger" means a craving or urgent need for food or a specific nutrient. A prolonged physical hunger, if not satisfied, can lead to malnutrition or even death. A physical hunger produces a desire to meet the need to feed our bodies. We generally go on a mission to find food with a greater sense of urgency when hungry. In the midst of intense physical hunger, locating food moves toward the top of the priority list. Cravings start to develop. The word "crave" means "to ask for earnestly; to want greatly; to yearn for."[1]

How does a spiritual hunger affect us? A hunger within our hearts for Jesus causes us to seek Him with even a greater sense of urgency. Seeking Him moves to the top of the priority list. Passivity can no longer be tolerated nor is there any comfort in mediocrity. A continual hunger for Jesus causes us to long for Him and seek Him in a way that is not passive but very purposeful. As we continually draw near to Jesus, He continually draws near to us, and we in turn desire Him even more (James 4:8). It then becomes a cycle of reciprocated love that produces a passion for our Lord Jesus Christ.

> *Psalms 63:1, "O God, thou art my God; early will I seek thee: my soul thirsteth for thee, my flesh longeth for thee in a dry and thirsty land, where no water is."*
>
> *Psalms 42:1-2, "As the hart panteth after the water brooks, so panteth my soul after thee, O God. My soul thirsteth for God, for the living God: when shall I come and appear before God?"*

As Christians, it is important that we examine ourselves for evidence of a true hunger for God. If there is a hunger for

God, it is important that we allow it to be sustained through committed prayer, worship and meditation on His word. If we examine ourselves and don't find evidence of a true hunger we must position ourselves to allow Him to work in us. The scripture tells us, "For it is God which worketh in you both to will and to do of His good pleasure" (Philippians 2:13). It is God that works a hunger in our hearts for Him. As we petition Him for change within us and we consistently and diligently position ourselves in a place of worship and prayer, He will work within us the change we so desire. Diligence is important, as the Lord has promised to reward those that diligently seek Him (Hebrews 11:6).

THE HEART OF OUR FATHER

The Bible gives clear evidence of what things are on the heart of our heavenly Father. In His word He speaks of the poor, the widows, and the fatherless. He has a love for the world and sent His only son Jesus to die for the sins of the world (John 3:16). In this following passage, in the book of John, Jesus made it clear to Peter what was on His heart:

John 21:15-17, "So when they had dined, Jesus saith to Simon Peter, Simon, son of Jonas, lovest thou Me more than these? He saith unto him, Yea, Lord; thou knowest that I love thee. He saith unto him, Feed my lambs. He saith to him again the second time, Simon, son of Jonas, lovest thou me? He saith unto him, Yea, Lord; thou knowest that I love thee. He saith unto him, Feed my sheep. He saith unto him the third time, Simon, son of Jonas, lovest thou me? Peter was grieved because He said unto him the third time, Lovest thou me? And he said unto him, Lord, thou knowest all things; thou knowest that I love thee. Jesus saith unto him, Feed my sheep."

Through the word of God we see the caring heart of Jesus regarding His sheep; sheep being God's people. On three occasions, He told Peter to feed His sheep, but prior to doing that He questioned Peter about the love that he had for Him. Could Peter truly say that he loved Jesus and not be willing to feed the sheep?

Jesus was making a correlation between loving Him and caring for the sheep. As is evidenced in the book of Acts, Peter not only fed the sheep but boldly preached the gospel resulting in multitudes coming into the Kingdom of God. He suffered persecution for the sake of the One he loved. What will the church do for the love of their Lord? It is important that the church understand what is on the heart of the Father. The heart of the Father is revealed through intimate prayer, worship and meditation on His word. We, the church, must allow our hearts to align with His heart. The church must FIRST love Jesus fervently and seek Him as the first order of ministry. God has commissioned the church, and just as He called Peter, we must respond with a heart of love and submission.

A Compassionate Heart

A heart of compassion is characteristic of our Lord, and as spiritual offspring, it must be a characteristic of us, His people. The word compassion means "a sympathetic consciousness of others distress together with a desire to alleviate it."[2] Based on this definition, the church must have a sympathetic consciousness of the needs of others with a desire to minister to those needs. People have many needs which include salvation and deliverance, love, food, clothing, shelter, etc. Love for the Father, coupled with a love and compassion for those that are in need, will compel the church to respond.

> *I John 3:17-18, "But whoso hath this world's good, and seeth his brother have need, and shutteth up his bowels of compassion from him, how dwelleth the love of God in him?" My little children, let us not love in word, neither in tongue; but in deed and in truth."*

CONCLUSION

The commission given to the church through the apostles to preach the gospel was never intended to be a burden, dreaded task, or assignment for a select few. The mandate must be fulfilled as millions upon millions of people have yet to hear the gospel even once. In the book of Acts, Peter and other apostles, after being threatened and told not to preach the gospel, rejoiced in that they were counted worthy to suffer shame for the sake of Jesus (Acts 5:41). Their willingness to suffer for the sake of Jesus gives us a clear indication of the degree of love the apostles had for Him.

It was love that caused God the Father to send His Son to be crucified for the sins of the world. The Bible tells us that God *SO LOVED* the world that He *GAVE* His only begotten Son (John 3:16). It will be through a great love for Jesus, and a love for souls, birthed through a continual and intimate fellowship with the Lord that will cause preaching and sharing the gospel to be a joy, a pleasure and a privilege. In the midst of seeking the Lord continually He will work in us a desire to do of His good pleasure (Philippians 2:13). Let us seek Him continually, long for Him, and thirst for Him that He may work within us a passionate love for Him that produces love and compassion for the lost. Let us fulfill the mandate Jesus has given His church.

Reflection

1. What compelled our heavenly Father to send His Son to die on the cross for the sins of the world?

2. Is it possible to love Jesus with all your heart, He being the *first love*, while at the same time not having a concern for unbelievers?

3. If after self-assessment you come to the conclusion that Jesus is no longer the *first love* in your life, and that zeal and passion for God is lacking, what should you do?

4. What does it mean to have compassion?

5. Are you willing to share the gospel message with those in need of salvation?

●

Reference

1. Merriam Webster Online Dictionary, http://www.merriam.com
2. Ibid

-Two-
THE APOSTOLIC MANDATE
THE ROLE OF THE BELIEVER

FOUNDATION

God has commissioned the church to proclaim the gospel message, teach all nations, and make disciples. We know that the church is not a building but the Body of Christ. Therefore if you are a member of the Body of Christ, Jesus has commissioned YOU. The word commissioned means "to appoint or assign to a task or function." God has appointed His people to the awesome task of "teaching all Nations" and of being a "witness" to the uttermost part of the earth (Matthew 28:19, Acts 1:8). It is important that every believer, from the very young to the very old, understands the gospel message and can communicate the message effectively. Believers are called to be able to give an answer to those who want to know the reason for their hope and trust in Jesus Christ (I Peter 3:15). *Every* Christian must know that they are God's representative in the earth and that He wants to use His people to lead souls into His Kingdom.

EVANGELISM

One of the ways the gospel message is communicated is through evangelism.

What is evangelism? Evangelism is "the winning or revival of personal commitments to Christ."[1]

I would like to define evangelism as, *"Communicating the gospel through various means for the purpose of leading an individual into a personal commitment to Christ."* The means of communication may vary as directed by the Holy Spirit and God is unlimited in His methods.

What is the gospel message? This message is the good news that God has provided a way of freedom from the bondage and penalty of sin and the promise of eternal life through faith in His Son Jesus Christ.

Evangelism is the method by which the message of reconciliation is communicated to the world.

What does it mean to be reconciled? To reconcile means to reestablish a close relationship after resolution of differences. God's plan since the fall of man, beginning with Adam, has been that man be restored in right relationship with Him because man as a sinner is separated from God.

Those who have been reconciled to God are called to be the ministers of reconciliation. As ambassadors of Christ, God's people have been appointed by Him to be His personal, officially authorized representative to the unbeliever.

> *II Corinthians 5:18, "And all things are of God, who hath reconciled us to himself by Jesus Christ, and hath given to us the ministry of reconciliation."*

NEW TESTAMENT MODELS OF EVANGELISM

There are biblical examples of evangelism which can be found in the gospels and in the book of Acts. Mass evangelism and personal evangelism are demonstrated. Both Jesus and His followers employed both methods. Mass evangelism allows a larger audience to be reached and has been the method by which the modern church has become most accustomed. This method is often seen when the invitation to accept Jesus as Lord and to repent is extended to an audience and the one extending the invitation is expecting a response. The practice of personal evangelism (one-on-one evangelism) has not appeared consistently on a broad scale amongst believers although this method has been proven to be most effective.

Jesus Ministered to Individuals
- Jesus ministered to Zacchaeus — Luke 19:5-9
- Jesus ministered to the Samaritan woman — John 4:6-29
John 39-41

Jesus Ministered to the Multitudes
- Jesus ministered to the multitude and fed 5000 — Luke 9:11-17

Early Church Ministry
- Mass Evangelism:
3000 respond after Peter's sermon — Acts 2:37-41
- Mass Evangelism:
5000 respond after Peter's sermon — Acts 4:1-4
- Multitudes saved
after Paul and Barnabas preach — Acts 14:1

MOTIVATION TO REACH NON-CHRISTIANS

As believers, should our only reason for sharing the gospel and winning the lost be that we are commanded to do so? God has called us to be willing and obedient to His word. If we find that we are simply acting out of obligation when we share the gospel, this lack of motivation, willingness, or desire must be addressed in prayer. If a genuine love and compassion for the lost is not evident in our lives, we must humbly go before God and allow Him to work in us. The scripture says, "For it is God which worketh in you both to will and to do of His good pleasure" Philippians 2:13. God works in us as we seek Him in prayer and submit to Him. In and through our daily devotions and times of intimate worship, God works in us a greater love for Him and love for the lost. We cannot "work up" a burden for lost souls. As we pray and cry out for souls in intercession, He works in us the love and compassion that will compel us to share the gospel.

Jesus is our Lord and example. We must endeavor to be more like Him. In Matthew 9:36, the Bible tells us that Jesus was moved with compassion as He looked upon the multitudes. John 3:16 says, "For God so loved the world, that He gave His only begotten Son, that whosoever believeth in Him should not perish, but have everlasting life." As we examine this familiar scripture, we see that God was compelled by love when He sent Jesus into the earth. Jesus went to the cross and stayed on the cross because He was compelled by love. He rose from the dead triumphant and lives at the right hand of the Father making intercession for the Saints because of love (Hebrews 7:22-25). We must have love and compassion, even as our Lord has, to effectively minister the word of God and lead the unsaved into relationship with Jesus Christ.

HINDRANCES TO WITNESSING OR SHARING THE GOSPEL

Before we move on to the next chapter, let us address some things that hinder many Christians from sharing the gospel with unbelievers. In order to be more effective in evangelistic ministry, we must be willing to address various areas that cause us to draw back from witnessing. As we pray and bring these matters before the Lord, and we're honest about the issues that hinder us, God will help us with those areas of weakness so that we can be most effective for Him.

FEAR AND INTIMIDATION
Whether you are facing fear of rejection, confrontation, appearing foolish, not knowing what to say, not knowing how to respond to tough questions, or fear of persecution, etc. – know that these fears are not of God. When we fear we are not walking in faith. We must believe that God has anointed us and equipped us for ministry. The Bible tells us that we have not been given a spirit of fear, but of power, and of love, and of a sound mind (II Timothy 1:7). If we examine the scripture reference in II Timothy in its context, we will see that Paul was encouraging Timothy to be fearless in the face of persecution. The apostles prayed for boldness in the face of being threatened (Acts 4:29). Did these apostles of the early church have to confront fear? They would have no need to pray for boldness if they had not been confronted with fear. In the face of fear, we must confront it, then pray and trust God to give us boldness as we take courageous steps for Him.

LACK OF DEVOTION - PERSONAL PRAYER LIFE
Unless we abide in Christ consistently, we as Christians can become distracted and not very focused nor interested in things that are on God's heart. It's only through abiding in Jesus and seeking Him first that we develop a spiritual appetite for spiritual things. As we grow in our love for Jesus more and more each day, we have even a greater desire to serve Him and willingness to give of ourselves to others.

SIN
It can be very difficult for a believer to desire to encourage someone else to repent and receive Jesus while yet practicing sin. When we sin and refuse to repent, we are walking in rebellion against God. We must be quick to repent of sin and willing to walk free from sin. As Christians, the Bible tells

us that we are no longer slaves to sin (Romans 6:16-18). Repenting of sin and renewing our relationship with Jesus will cause us to come to the place where we desire to share the gospel and see others walk in freedom from sin as well.

ENTANGLED IN THE CARES OF THIS LIFE

It seems in this fast paced world we live in, everyone is busy all the time. Husbands, wives; single men and women and even children sometimes say they are busy. So when do we have time to minister to the lost? Most of us don't seem to have a lot of spare time, but we do make time (prioritize) for the things that are important to us. When we "seek ye first the Kingdom of God...." we are more willing to make God's desires priority. God can show us how to prioritize our busy schedules if we acknowledge Him when we plan our days or weeks ahead. We are not only sons and daughters of God but soldiers in a spiritual battle. The war is between the kingdom of darkness and the Kingdom of Light. The scripture in II Timothy 2:4 says, "No man that warreth entangleth himself with the affairs of this life; that he may please Him who hath chosen him to be a soldier." It is not God's desire that His church become so entangled in the cares of this life that the winning of souls become low priority. We must give ourselves to God's priorities as our lives are no longer our own, but we have been purchased through the precious blood of Jesus Christ.

> *Galatians 2:20, "I am crucified with Christ: nevertheless I live; yet not I, but Christ liveth in me: and the life which I now live in the flesh I live by the faith of the Son of God, who loved me, and gave himself for me."*

LACK OF PREPARATION

There are times God may set up divine appointments where

we have opportunities to witness or share the gospel in our everyday lives. Sometimes we may feel very inadequate when we know we have not given sufficient time to prayer, study, or meditation on key scriptures. While we must depend upon the Holy Spirit and the grace of God as we minister in every situation regardless of the preparation, God has called us to study and to be ready.

II Timothy 2:15, "Study to shew thyself approved unto God, a workman that needeth not to be ashamed, rightly dividing the word of truth."

Evangelism is a lifestyle and as a result it is necessary to actively look for those opportunities to share, to pray for those opportunities daily, and expect God to set up divine appointments. These opportunities may come at work, with family, neighbors, or strangers. Evangelism is deliberate. We must deliberately pray for the lost, look for opportunities to witness, and prepare for divine appointments. Create a list of those people on your heart that need salvation. Lack of deliberate preparation to evangelize has caused the church to miss opportunities to win the lost. Let's prepare ourselves and expect to be used by God.

CONCLUSION

Each individual within the body of Christ has been called to be a witness and share the gospel. This heavenly calling is to be considered a command rather than an option. Although it is a command to "go into all the world and preach the gospel" the motivation for sharing the good news should come from a love for the Lord (Mark 12:30). An "all of the heart" kind of love for God will produce a love for people and a desire to see the unsaved come into a relationship with the Lord Jesus Christ and be changed.

Fulfilling the heavenly mandate can be a challenge, since so many things come to hinder evangelistic efforts, but these challenges can be overcome as a commitment is made to life transforming prayer and study of the Word. Let us, the people of God, commit ourselves to growing in our love for God, then from a place of love for our Lord, be a witness for Christ as a part of a Christian lifestyle.

REFLECTION

1. What is evangelism?

2. Name at least three hindrances to sharing the gospel?

3. What does it mean to be reconciled to God?

4. What is the number one hindrance in your personal life, if any, from sharing the gospel? What scripture(s) can you use to help you overcome this hindrance?

•

REFERENCE
1. Merriam Webster Online Dictionary, http://www.merriam.com

-Three-
PERSONAL EVANGELISM
INTRODUCING PEOPLE TO JESUS

FOUNDATION

Through one-on-one evangelism, or personal evangelism, we are given the opportunity to share the gospel with individuals face to face. Many Christians find it difficult to share their faith with strangers or even with those familiar to them. Some of those fears or feelings of intimidation can come from feelings of inadequacy or being unprepared as mentioned in the previous chapter. God has called His people to study and meditate upon His word. We must know what we believe and why we believe it.

It is important that we are not only able to give an answer to those that inquire about our commitment and hope in Jesus Christ, but we must also know *how* to share the gospel message in a way that is easily understood. We are called to introduce unbelievers to the one and only true God and Savior, the Lord Jesus Christ, and help them understand their need for Him. The unbeliever must come to know that they are in need of a Savior as a result of realizing their sin in light of God's word. We are not introducing them to a religious practice, with doctrine and practices devoid of spiritual encounters, but we are first introducing them to a real, living Jesus who once walked among us in the flesh. This same Jesus loves them, and desires a relationship with them.

The mindset of some unbelievers regarding Christianity is that it is just another religion with rules to follow or doctrine to understand, and they don't see the need for it. There are many things that set Christianity apart from all other religions, but there are a couple of very important things to note. One important point is that Jesus is a _resurrected_ Lord and Savior. Many have sought to discount the resurrection for it is through the resurrection that God's power is revealed. The second important point to note is that our God is not an impersonal God that chooses to Lord over His people through intimidation, but a God who extends to His people an opportunity to have a personal relationship with Him. Jesus, who is God and the Head of the church, desires to be in fellowship with His sons and daughters and to reveal Himself to His people.

The purpose of this chapter is to bring clarity to those things that are important to communicate to an unbeliever. What are the more important points that need to be communicated to the unsaved in a gospel presentation? We will address these points within this chapter.

It's important that the message is clear and that the soul-winner stays focused in conversation. An unbeliever can feel almost overwhelmed when a soul-winner gives ten scriptures, and asks ten questions in ten minutes. Knowing key scriptures, having answers to anticipated responses, and being sensitive to the direction of the Holy Spirit helps the soul-winner to be more prepared, more focused and stay in control of the conversation. Sure every situation is never exactly the same, and every possible response may not always be anticipated, but the Holy Spirit is our partner in ministry and He leads us in every situation. Being prepared and being Spirit led is of the utmost importance. The more we share the gospel and trust God to lead us, the more sensitive we become to the voice of God. A dialogue may start at a certain point, or take a different course, but certain main points need to be clear to the unbeliever as we share the gospel with them. The way these points are brought forth and the method of delivery will vary as the Holy Spirit leads. In short, the unbeliever needs to know he is a sinner and that sin brings death. He must know that God provided a solution: forgiveness and eternal life comes through faith in the Lord Jesus, and he must decide to receive or reject Jesus as Lord. In each and every situation we must trust that the Holy Spirit will speak through us, teach us, and continually give us His strategies.

FAITH TO BE A WITNESS
The grace and giftings that we receive from God to fulfill the commission are received by faith. When we ask anything of God in prayer, we receive what we ask for by faith. God acts in response to faith. We must believe that God has equipped us for the task of sharing the gospel.

EVANGELISM AND THE ROLE OF THE HOLY SPIRIT
The Holy Spirit is at work through us and partnering with us in ministry. It is the Holy Spirit that does the work as we submit to the will of God. It is the Holy Spirit that draws the unbeliever, convicts them of sin, and brings them to the point of decision for Christ. Let us ask God for boldness and trust the Holy Spirit to confirm the word as we step out in faith and obedience to be a witness for Him.

God at Work in You
- God works in us — Philippians 2:13
- God has not given us a spirit of fear — II Timothy 1:7
- Greater is He that is in you — I John 4:4

The Holy Spirit Equipping the Believer

- Power to be a witness   Acts 1:8
- God speaks through us   Matthew 10:19-20
- The Holy Spirit testifies of Jesus   John 15:26
- Comes through you
  to reprove the world of sin   John 16:8

PRESENTATION OF THE GOSPEL MESSAGE

The gospel is not "good news" to the unsaved person unless he knows his spiritual state and need for a Savior. It is our job as ambassadors of Christ to present the gospel in such a way that the unbeliever recognizes that he is a sinner, that the wages of sin is death (consequences of sin). We need to explain that Jesus has made provisions for forgiveness, and that he must make a choice to reject or accept it. When the sinner does not make a choice for Christ, he has made a choice to remain a sinner and receive the eternal consequences for sin.

There are many cases where we find the unsaved person knows he is guilty of sin but needs to know he can be forgiven. Some may have given up on believing that forgiveness and freedom from sin, bondage, guilt and shame are possible. In these cases, the gospel is a message of hope and good news for them as they hear that God loves them and has made a way for them to be free from sin and forgiven.

MAN'S UNIVERSAL PROBLEM

Romans 3:23, "For all have sinned, and come short of the glory of God."

This verse shows that we all have done things that are considered sin before God. It's very important that we use scripture when sharing the gospel, but we must also explain what that scripture means and be mindful to simplify scriptural language. This verse must be made personal for the individual who hears the word. The scripture says that ALL have sinned, and the sinner must know that he has *personally* sinned before God. If the individual has difficulty understanding that he has sinned, then the individual should be challenged to see his sin as it relates to the word of God and not to the standards of modern society. The word of God tells us what things are considered sin, and in this modern age, it should not be assumed that people know what God calls sin.

Scriptures to Reference:

- Ten Commandments   Exodus 20:2-17
- The unrighteous will not
  see heaven   I Corinthians 6:9-10
- God hates pride, a lying tongue,
  sowing of discord, etc.   Proverbs 6:16-19

Through the word of God the sinner can come to understand that he has committed sin and is guilty before God.

THE PENALTY OF SIN

Romans 6:23, "For the wages of sin is death; but the gift of God is eternal life through Jesus Christ our Lord."

This verse explains the penalty for sin. Once it is clear that the sinner stands guilty before God, the individual needs to know that sin has a death penalty. The death penalty is eternal damnation. To help the individual to understand the seriousness of the final judgment, good scriptures to reference are Revelation 20:12, 15.

The good news for the sinner that realizes he is guilty before God is that Jesus has provided a way for him to be forgiven and to inherit the gift of eternal life.

GOD'S PROVISION FOR MAN
Romans 5:8, "God commendeth His love toward us, in that, while we were yet sinners, Christ died for us."

This verse explains that God has made a way for the sinner to be forgiven of his sins. It's important that the individual understands the great love that Jesus has for him personally. The individual must know that Jesus so loved him that He has made a way for him to be forgiven. THIS is good news when the sinner knows he's guilty and has a desire to be forgiven.

THE SALVATION PROCESS
Romans 10:9-10, "If thou shalt confess with thy mouth the Lord Jesus, and shalt believe in thine heart that God has raised Him from the dead, thou shalt be saved. For with the heart man believeth unto righteousness; and with the mouth confession is made unto salvation."

This verse explains the salvation process. The scripture says that the individual must confess the "LORD Jesus," which means a submission to Jesus as Lord and a surrender of his life to Jesus Christ. The individual must know that Jesus is a risen Lord who calls all men to repent and knocks upon the door of his heart that he may open up and receive Him (John 1:12, Revelation 3:20). This process involves the will and heart of the individual.

Confession is an important part of the salvation process.

Once the individual repents and receives Jesus as Lord, the new believer must begin to identify himself before others as one who has made a decision to surrender to the Lordship of Jesus Christ and follow His word (Matthew 10:32-33).

GOD'S PROMISE TO MAN
Romans 10:13, "Whosoever will call upon the name of the Lord shall be saved."

This verse explains that God promises salvation to all those that call upon Him out of a sincere heart and ask forgiveness of sin. It's important that the new believer come to understand that salvation is not only being saved from eternal damnation but freedom from the bondage of sin and the inheritance of the blessing of God's healing, provision and protection.

A CLEAR MESSAGE
Since many unbelievers do not understand certain biblical terms or language, these things must be considered and remembered when sharing the gospel message. We must present the gospel in simple terms and talk in a language that's easily understood. A good exercise: try practicing the gospel presentation with a fellow Christian while not using biblical terms that an unbeliever may not understand. Remember to keep it simple but grounded in the word of God. Words like saved, unsaved, born again, repentance, reconciliation, etc. may not be clear to the unbeliever or unchurched. Even if the individual has heard of such words, the full meaning may not be clearly understood.

PREPARING FOR PERSONAL EVANGELISM
Evangelism is a Lifestyle
Some Christians think of participating in evangelism efforts mainly when an organized outreach is planned through the

church or missions organization. They might not think of deliberately sharing the gospel again until the next evangelistic event is scheduled. Evangelism is not an outreach event, but is a lifestyle. It is simply intended to be a part of life for a Christian, or at least it should be. Evangelism should be a part of Christian living just as much as reading the Bible and prayer would be expected of Christians. In order to become more prepared for evangelistic encounters, the mindset about evangelism must be changed. The Body of Christ must allow God to renew their mind and change their ways of thinking about this area of ministry. The renewing of the mind process begins with prayer and *study* of the word; particularly those verses dealing with evangelism and winning the lost (Romans 12:2). We must prepare ourselves to be ready whenever God provides the opportunity. We must also allow ourselves to be sensitive enough to the Spirit of God to recognize an opportunity to share while praying for boldness and courage and not willing to run from a God given opportunity. In the book of Acts there were times where conversions occurred as God divinely set up the encounters (Acts 8:26-40). God wants to give each of us divine encounters and opportunities. Let us pray and ask Him for these divine appointments daily. Take the prayer challenge!

STUDY THE WORD
It is important that we study God's word and seek Him for understanding. We don't fully understand something until we can teach what we know. It is important that we have knowledge of the word of God and can explain it in a way easily understood by others.

If someone who had no knowledge of Jesus asked, "Who is Jesus," can you provide an answer based on scripture? If someone says they believe in a God but don't believe in

Jesus, but believes being a good person is enough to go to heaven, do you have a scripture based response? What scriptures would you use to testify of Jesus and show them the true way of salvation? These are questions we are better prepared to respond to when we regularly study God's word. Let us study, pray for understanding, grace and anointing from God to be able to easily share the Word of Life with the unbeliever.

THE IMPORTANCE OF A PLAN

God gives us strategies in ministry. Just as we receive strategies from God on how to teach and train believers within the church, He also gives us strategies on how to win the lost, those outside the church. The Bible tells us "…he that winneth souls is wise" (Proverbs 11:30). There is wisdom from God available to us on how to present the gospel in any given situation and wisdom on how to reach the masses. There have been various means given to us by God to reach the lost, some of which we will discuss in later chapters. We must allow God to prepare us to reach the unbeliever with strategies relevant to this season and generation. When we know that God has prepared us through our diligently seeking Him and allowing His Spirit to train us, we'll walk in more confidence and boldness. We'll operate in wisdom by keeping the conversation focused when ministering to the unbeliever and faith by trusting the Holy Spirit to direct us. Preparation and strategy are important elements in effective evangelistic ministry.

Many Christians feel as if they are not sure where to begin when presenting the gospel message. It's important that we listen to the voice of the Holy Spirit to get instructions and strategy. As we open up our mouths to share, we must trust God by faith to fill it (Jeremiah 1:9). Some examples of opening questions are below and may work in certain settings or cultural environments. These examples of questions are not presented as a rule or required method but presented as tools that can be used as a springboard to enter into conversation with someone on spiritual matters.

Opening Question 1:
Can I have a moment of your time to ask you a question?

This opening question is a question where consent is first sought and allows the individual to decide if they have time or want to engage in conversation with you. If the person gives you consent, you have been given an open door to share with them as God directs. It's important to be clear and share with simplicity. It is also important to ask a few questions that will provide an understanding of what it is the person believes before beginning to share and making assumptions. Understanding where the individual is in their understanding and relationship with God helps you, the soul-winner, to know where to begin.

There will be cases where the above question is not appropriate and God may lead you to be direct and just begin to speak to the unbeliever what God has given you to share. Sensitivity to the spirit of God is key.

Opening Question 2:
If you died today,
do you believe that you are going to heaven?

If the individual says "yes" to the question of heaven, then ask them to explain why they believe they are going to heaven. Listen carefully and allow the Holy Spirit to give you insight on how to give a response. Eternal life comes through Jesus Christ (Romans 6:23). Remember, if the individual does not have Jesus, they don't have the promise of heaven since eternal life is the gift of God through faith in our Savior Jesus Christ. This is an opportunity to share the gospel truth and explain how they can have the assurance of heaven.

Opening Question 3:
Do you identify yourself as a Christian?

Some might just say, "no." If "no" is the response, ask them if they are willing to share what they believe a Christian is or if they ever thought of being a Christian. In some cases, you might find the person may have once considered themselves Christian, but became disinterested in the Christian faith and sought out other religions. Others may have become disillusioned due to disappointments or through observing what they believe to be hypocrisy by those who call themselves Christian. Some may have been raised in a household where their family was of another faith such as Jewish, Muslim, Buddhist, or Hindu and being Christian was looked upon unfavorably. Whatever the case, allow yourself to listen first while seeking an opportunity to share truth. The truth must be based on the scripture when addressing any questions or misconceptions about the Christian faith.

If the individual does believe that he or she is a Christian, allow them to explain what they believe a Christian is. If the answer is incorrect, ask the individual if they would allow you to share what a Christian is based on a Bible based definition. Many people often explain what a Christian does instead of what is Christian is. Use this opportunity to emphasize that doing "works" does not make one a Christian, since salvation is not based on works (Ephesians 2:8-9). Others may respond to the above question by saying they have not thought of becoming a Christian and are not sure what to believe about Christianity. A response that has been given quite frequently by non-believers with no religious affiliation is, "I am not Christian, but consider myself a spiritual person." Take the time to listen and understand what that means to them and allow the Holy Spirit to give you a response. This is an opportunity to share truth and dispel myths of the "universal God with many paths to salvation" mindset and teaching. Salvation only comes through Jesus Christ (Acts 4:12).

PRAYER AND EVANGELISM
Prayer is very important and vital as it pertains to the fruitfulness of evangelistic efforts. Demonic forces have set up roadblocks and hindrances to keep the unbeliever in spiritual darkness and to keep the Christian from reaching those in need of salvation. Unless the hindrances are confronted and removed through prayer, the unbeliever may remain in spiritual darkness and bondage, and evangelistic efforts may be frustrated. The Bible tells us that no man comes unto the Father unless the Spirit of the Lord draws him (John 14:6). We must therefore pray that God would have mercy and draw the unbeliever unto Himself. If these hindrances to salvation are not confronted through prayer, and the Holy Spirit is not drawing him, the unbeliever has no ability to perceive what the Christian is sharing, nor the ability to repent and receive Jesus as Lord and Savior. Through prayer, God gives His church directions or specific instructions. Through prayer, Christians "stand in the gap" for the unsaved and through prayer, God reveals demonic

strongholds or hindrances to evangelism. We, the church, are to exercise our delegated authority to confront demonic strongholds through prayer.

DISCIPLESHIP - YOUR RESPONSIBILITY

Once a person gives their life to the Lord Jesus Christ it is just the beginning. It is the responsibility of the soul-winner to follow-up with the new believer and support them in their new journey or new life in Christ. It is also the responsibility of the soul-winner to lead the new believer through a discipleship process or in some cases to find a more appropriate person to disciple them. Jesus never called the church to simply make new believers only, but to make "disciples" of all nations. Jesus was our great example and master discipler. Disciples are made when mature Christians invest into the lives of new believers while allowing God to bring that new Christian to a place of maturity. Remember, the new believer has made a major decision, and in most cases has friends and family that may not be Christians. Their non-Christian friends may not understand nor respect the decision made by the new believer to follow Christ. There can be a lot of pressure by family, old friends, acquaintances, etc. to do things contrary to the word of God. The new believer needs to hear from YOU, be instructed in the word, and make new friends in the Body of Christ. So be friendly and embrace them as they are a part of the family of God.

The decision for Christ is just the beginning of their journey with God. The beginning stages in the development of a new believer are very important, just as the life of an infant can be fragile in early development. Intercede, pray for, and pray with the new believer. If the new believer is of the opposite sex, get a partner that can work alongside you in reaching out to this individual. Husband and wife ministry teams can be very supportive to one another in these situations. The new believer is not just another name to add to the "those that got saved today list" but is important and special in the eyes of God. What's important to God must be important to us as Christians. It's our responsibility as mature Christians to nurture the new believer. We should not want to be used in the birthing process of the new believer just to leave them on the birthing table alone with no nurturing, care, covering, direction, or spiritual food. More in depth teaching on discipleship is found in a later chapter.

CONCLUSION

As committed followers of Christ, it is very important we know what it is that we believe about Jesus Christ, the Bible and eternal life. We not only need to know the reason for the hope we have in Christ but be able to communicate clearly the message of the gospel. Allowing ourselves to be equipped to effectively share the gospel requires a commitment to study and diligence in preparation. Diligence and commitment will be rewarded by God and the fruit of it will be evident in our lives and ministry (Hebrews 11:6).

REFLECTION

1. Based on the section of "A Clear Message" in this chapter, write down two presentations given to two different "types" of people and scenarios without using biblical terms.

2. Examples of types of people: (1) You are ministering to a loved one; (2) alcoholic or illegal substance user; (3) the drug dealer who is enjoying illegal gain; (4) a person who goes to church regularly but isn't saved or committed to Christ; (5) a co-worker; and (6) an intellectual who does not believe he needs God, etc.

-Four-
SHARING A PERSONAL TESTIMONY

FOUNDATION
Anyone who is truly a born again Christian has a personal testimony of how Jesus Christ changed their life. A personal testimony of God's transforming power in the life of the Christian is a spiritual tool that can be used by God and an important part of evangelistic ministry.

In order to be most effective in sharing one's personal testimony, it is important to be sensitive to the Holy Spirit, conscious of the setting, the audience, cultural considerations, gender of the individual(s) and time limitations.

The purpose of this chapter is to outline a few important points to consider in sharing one's personal testimony. Jesus has called us to be "witnesses" for Him and the Holy Spirit has been sent to help us become even more effective at being a witness of our salvation through Jesus Christ to the "uttermost parts of the earth" (Acts 1:8).

THE POWER OF YOUR TESTIMONY
God anoints His people to share the gospel and to be a witness for Him. As Christians we are called to testify of the transforming power of Jesus Christ in word, action and character. Part of being a witness for Jesus is the sharing of our personal testimony. Whether

we share a few words that testify of our relationship with Jesus Christ and the truth of His word, or have an opportunity to share our personal testimony at length, it is important to be prepared when the Holy Spirit prompts us to do so.

Our personal testimony is powerful. Many people have come to accept Jesus after hearing a powerful testimony. Skeptics often try to challenge the validity of the Bible and its meaning. Those inspired to write the word of God are no longer alive to provide a personal testimony of its reality. Yet one's personal testimony and experience cannot be taken away because it is *personal* and you who testify is alive. A skeptic may try to question the source of an individual's transformation when hearing the testimony but only the one who testifies knows the details and reality of their personal story. In instances where an individual's life before and after salvation has been witnessed by those who have known them for some time, the evidence of a transformed life is a testimony in itself.

In John 4:5-42, we read the story of a Samaritan woman that encountered Jesus at Jacob's well. After she realized that she was speaking to the Messiah, she ran back to tell the people in her town. The Samaritan woman simply shared her testimony and many people believed as a result.

> *John 4:39, "And many of the Samaritans of that city believed on Him for the saying of the woman, which testified, He told me all that I ever did." (New King James Version)*

DEFINING TESTIMONY
A Greek word for a testimony is "maturia." Maturia is translated "witness" in many instances in the New Testament.

So, to give a testimony is to make a witness statement. The Greek word "martus" is the basis for the English word "martyr", who is one who bears witness by his death.[1] Christians are called to testify of Jesus even if acknowledging Him as God and Messiah could mean death.

The Webster New World Dictionary[2] defines testimony as "a statement made under oath to establish a fact; any declaration; any form of evidence; proof." So, through our personal testimony and experience of personal relationship with our Lord, we establish the fact that Jesus is real, that His word is true, and our transformed life is evidence or proof of God's transforming power.

CONSIDERING YOUR AUDIENCE

When sharing your personal testimony with an individual, and speaking of your experiences prior to salvation, focusing on or emphasizing experiences where the listener may be more apt to identify with can be very strategic. God will often give specific things to emphasize and share of our past experiences. For example, let's say the individual you are speaking with is an alcoholic. This person may really be encouraged to believe that Jesus will transform and deliver them if freedom from alcoholism happens to be a part of your testimony.

In cases where an individual or group may be of a different gender, different cultural or ethnic background such as Asian (Indian, Chinese, Malaysian, etc.), or perhaps Middle Eastern, it may not always be wise to freely share details of some past experiences as a part of your testimony such as sexual encounters, multiple marriages, or certain other experiences. Matters such as this may be considered by some cultures to be shameful and not to be spoken of even if it is a part of your testimony. Some people, who have not been long term residents in the United States, may find it hard to identify with some American cultural practices that may be immoral but seemingly accepted. Certain practices may not be widely or openly practiced or discussed in their native country. When ministering overseas, it is important to spend some time researching the culture before traveling to a particular country.

When sharing a testimony, we must make it clear that we were sinners in need of a Savior as evidenced by past sin, practices contrary to God and a stony heart. As we are led by the Holy Spirit, God will show us what key experiences to share in detail, or in brief, in order to show the listener that we were in need of salvation through Jesus Christ, even as all are in need of salvation since all have sinned (Romans 3:23).

As Christians today, all of us are daily in need of God's saving grace. Sin is not a cultural problem, it is a world problem, and most people can identify with committing sin at some point. As we are discerning and listening to our lead partner in ministry, the Holy Spirit, God will show us how to be most effective in giving our testimony in diverse situations and cultural settings.

AN EXERCISE IN SHARING A TESTIMONY
In the various opportunities we are given to share the gospel, we may have only a few minutes to share our testimony and the truth of God's word. In instances where we may have limited time, it is important to remember and be prepared to share our personal testimony concisely in three main parts, pre-salvation, salvation experience, and transformation.

As a part of this chapter you are encouraged to practice both a written and verbal personal testimony of your salvation experience. Your personal testimony in this exercise should be given the following time allotments:

- Pre-Salvation   30 seconds
- Salvation Experience   90 seconds
- Transformation   90 seconds

Remember to use words common to most people or words that can be easily understood. Many people are not familiar with certain biblical terms and do not know how to define such words as "born again" or "saved." Many people do understand words such as changed, transformed, made new, new heart, etc. Keep it simple and be Spirit led.

When sharing a testimony, although this lesson encourages preparation, the personal testimony should not sound like a script or Christian commercial. A love of Christ and joy of salvation should be evident as the testimony is shared. The person that hears the testimony needs to sense a faith and belief in God's love and transforming power.

PRE-SALVATION EXPERIENCE
As the pre-salvation experience is shared, life before salvation is explained as it relates to such things as the circumstances, actions, thoughts, mindsets, emotions or beliefs of your life before Christ. It is important that the testimony establishes the fact that there was a great need for Christ due to personal sin and a need for forgiveness and salvation; also a realization that the salvation which was needed only came through Jesus (Acts 4:12).

SALVATION EXPERIENCE
As the salvation experience is shared, the life changing

encounter with Jesus and the immediate changes that followed are explained.

TRANSFORMATION

As the transformation experience is shared, this is where the positive changes since salvation are highlighted. The benefits of the change and the reason for continued devotion to Christ along with faith in His word are explained.

JESUS OUR FOCUS

Jesus tells us in the word of God, "And I, if I be lifted up from the earth, will draw all men unto me" (John 12:32). In the context of this verse, Jesus is speaking of His eventual crucifixion on the cross where He was to be lifted up for so many to see. Yet even today the principle holds true, that if we lift up Jesus and exalt Him in testimony He will draw men unto himself.

As we share our testimony, we are not to lift up our pre-salvation experiences of sin in such a way as to glory in the memory of the sin nor appear proud of having such experiences. The main purpose of sharing the pre-salvation experience is to show why salvation was needed and how JESUS showed mercy and provided a way of forgiveness.

Our overall testimony needs to show the love, mercy, forgiveness, healing and deliverance of Jesus; show the power and provisions of Jesus, the joy of being in a relationship with Jesus and the eternal hope in Jesus. Jesus must be lifted up and be our focus as we testify.

CONCLUSION

It is important as believers that we know and not forget the power of our testimony. God has called His church to testify of Jesus to the world and so we must prepare ourselves for these divine opportunities. Most people are familiar with sharing their personal stories whether it relates to salvation or another life event that is very meaningful to them, but as we testify, the love, forgiveness, deliverance and blessings of Jesus must be at the core of the testimony. As we share our testimony out of love for and faith in Jesus Christ we trust that by faith God will open the spiritual ears of the hearer and use each encounter to impact and change lives.

REFLECTION

1. Why is it important to be clear and concise when sharing a testimony?

2. What are the possible consequences of not considering the audience when sharing a personal testimony?

3. What might be the reason for a believer highlighting their sin prior to salvation as if re-living the "glory days" of sin?

4. Is it possible to share a salvation testimony and not have Jesus as the main focus? Give an example.

•

REFERENCE

1. The Expanded Vines-Expository Dictionary of New Testament Words, Bethany House Publishers, 1984, pg. 1237
2. The Webster New World Dictionary, 1977, pg. 687

-Five-
CELL MINISTRY
EVANGELISM AND DISCIPLESHIP

FOUNDATION

The cell group is a gathering of a small group of people for the purpose of pastoral care, teaching the word of God, training for ministry, evangelism and spiritual edification. Its members consist of people who are committed to the local church and overall vision of the church. Unlike a bible study group where the main focus is teaching, the cell group is to provide training for its members with a goal of multiplication. Multiplication comes through evangelism, and discipleship is the process whereby new converts can make the transition to become mature Christians.

Through cell ministry, church members who may have been "spectators" in the local church have an opportunity to become more active members and build relationship with others. This happens more readily in a small group setting. In order for cell groups to continually grow and develop, the cell group must focus on seeking God first, building relationships within, reaching out to those outside of the group (non-Christians), and training new leaders. Through cell ministry, larger numbers of Christians receive more regular pastoral care, are trained for ministry, and are able to reach larger numbers of non-Christians.

Multiplication of cell groups in a neighborhood or region leads to community transformation as faith filled and spirit led disciples are multiplied, trained and equipped to bring change in their sphere of influence.

There are various topics that could be discussed in great detail in reference to cell ministry, but this chapter will focus on evangelism and discipleship within and outside the cell group.

VISION FOR MULTIPLICATION

Habakkuk 2:2, "And the LORD answered me, and said, Write the vision, and make it plain upon tables, that he may run that readeth it."

The vision for multiplication through evangelism must be clear to the cell group members. The cell leader is responsible for bringing the vision before the people and making sure each member understands it. When the vision is understood, and the cell group members embrace it, then the people can run with the vision. When there is clear vision, vision produces faith, faith then produces passion, and passion produces commitment that results in action. Evangelism (outreach) and discipleship is the means by which multiplication comes. Each member must reach out to non-Christians and have a lifestyle of evangelism. Each member is responsible for nurturing new believers and helping them grow into mature believers.

The church has become so accustomed to being "inwardly" focused that it is often challenging to get church members to remember to be "outwardly" focused. Bringing attention to the vision for multiplication on a weekly basis can help people adjust their mindsets about church and ministry. There are many needs that are addressed within the cell group on a weekly basis. Often times addressing the needs within can almost overshadow the importance of addressing the needs without or outside the cell group. Is the church too busy to grow? Unless the cell group leader and its members remember to be "outwardly" focused as well as care for those within, there is likely to be very little evangelism and then multiplication becomes slow.

SETTING GOALS FOR MULTIPLICATION

It is important to set evangelistic goals for the cell group. Goal setting helps the cell leader and members stay focused and make the best use of time. Goals are not meant to make people feel under pressure to meet timelines, but having goals help the work of the ministry move forward. Often when goals are not set, there may be a tendency for people to procrastinate or put important matters aside for "later." When is later? This word can have a very broad meaning and can refer to tomorrow, next week, next month or even next year. Setting evangelistic goals for three months, six months or twelve months ahead will help the cell members maintain an outward focus and have a more accurate measure of progress. Goals can and should be re-assessed over a period of time. God honors our petitions through prayer. Psalms 2:8 says, "Ask of me, and I shall give thee the heathen for thine inheritance, and the uttermost parts of the earth for thy possession." The cell group should pray concerning their evangelistic goals, act in faith through outreach, and believe God to give the increase.

PLANS FOR OUTREACH AND EVANGELISM

In order for the cell group to move forward in the ministry of evangelism, there must be short and long term plans for outreach. Goals are tied into the vision and provide timelines, but plans provide steps on HOW to reach those goals. Who are those targeted for salvation? Are they co-workers, relatives, neighbors, or acquaintances? Are there plans to reach the community where the cell group is located? These are important questions and having a plan is also important. We know that we can do nothing outside of the Lord's help and guidance, but as we seek Him for direction and carry out His plans, then we shall succeed. As the cell group seeks God together for evangelistic strategy, it is important to be reminded of the scripture in Psalms 37:5 which says "Commit thy way unto the LORD; trust also in Him; and He shall bring it to pass."

FRIENDSHIP EVANGELISM

What is friendship evangelism? This type of evangelism takes place as a result of developing a relationship with a non-Christian over a period of time. The soul-winner gains trust with the non-Christian as a result of their willingness to show genuine love, build relationship, and be a friend. This type of friendship is different from that which is established between two believers, as when two people are walking in the light of Christ, but it can be similar in that the Christian is willing to show genuine love and compassion to the unbeliever. A show of love and compassion should be in all relationships established among the body of Christ as this shows the world that we are Christ's disciples, but the non-Christian should also see and sense genuine love and care from the Christian (John 13:35). Building these relationships can take several weeks, months, or in some cases years, but friendship evangelism is known to be one of the most effective methods of evangelism. It has been said that approximately seven out of ten church members are Christians today as a result of a relative, friend, or acquaintance being an influence.

We live in a more impersonal society within the U.S., particularly in urban areas, and often people are conditioned to be impersonal and don't even realize it. Many people simply don't want to get involved in other people's lives, even some Christians. Some people feel like they have enough friends and simply don't have time for new ones. Present relationships and commitments may seem so demanding that the idea of adding a new friend seems too emotionally exhausting. Whatever the reasons are for Christians not reaching out to the unbeliever in love and friendship, it does not exclude the church from the mandate to reach the world with the gospel. Non-Christians from nations around the world are "in our own backyard," so to speak. The church has the opportunity to reach all people by showing love and being friendly.

It becomes easier to invite someone to a cell group meeting or church service when a relationship has been established with the individual. It almost seems that the Christian "earns the right to invite" after trust has been established. When building a relationship, make sure that the motive is truly to be a friend and extend love and not to simply add another name on the "people who just got saved" list. People can sense when certain Christians are genuine or have ulterior motives for the relationship. There are people with many needs around us and some are simply lonely. Regardless of the personality type of any given Christian, love and compassion should compel the Christian to reach out to those in need. Spiritual sensitivity will allow for key opportunities to be recognized.

So how do we take first steps toward building a relationship with individuals such as colleagues, acquaintances, neighbors, etc.? Here are a few ideas:

- Go to lunch with a co-worker
- Go to the mall with the old friend or acquaintance with whom you've been out of touch

- Go fishing with your neighbor that loves to fish
- Invite the neighbor over to the family barbecue or offer to send over a plate
- Make yourself available when there is a need where you can provide assistance

COMMUNITY OUTREACH

The church community, the people that make up the church, have not always been actively visible within the community. Many churches hold worship services behind the four walls on Sundays and conclude with no plans to engage the surrounding community. Yet, there are needs to be met within the community that God may have the church to address. Government led outreach programs are helpful for those that are in need and struggling with addiction, involved in violence, or simply need counseling or shelter but these programs don't address the spiritual needs of the individual. People need provision to have their natural and physical needs met, but they also need the spiritual transformation and blessings that comes as a result of salvation. When the church reaches out and gets involved in what is happening in the community, or contributes to meeting the natural and spiritual needs of the people, trust is established and local churches are viewed by more in the mainstream or secular world as being an active and vital part of building the community.

So what can the church and the individuals within the church do to build relationships within the community?

Here are a few ideas:
- A group of Christian men play basketball or some other sport in the neighborhood park and get to know the young men that come out to play daily

or weekly. This may lead to establishing sport leagues and building long term relationships with teens and young adults
- Attendance at a Neighborhood Watch or community policing meeting allows church members to meet neighbors and become more aware of happenings within the community
- The cell group organizes a "pray for our community" meeting with the neighbors that address the prayer needs or concerns of the community
- Needs within the neighborhood are identified– such as the widow who needs her hedges trimmed around her home, and the church member does the work for no charge
- A weekly tutoring class is established in the community, led by Christians, giving them the opportunity to meet parents and children while helping the children develop needed skills

SALVATION IS JUST THE BEGINNING

The church and the angels rejoice over one sinner that repents and receives Jesus as Lord and Savior (Luke 15:10). Weekly in church services sinners repent of sins and express a desire to surrender their lives to Jesus. During evangelistic crusades or outreaches great numbers of people come to the altar, repent of sins, and make a decision to follow Christ. Often the number of souls who expressed a desire to follow Jesus are counted after these evangelistic events and testimonials are given to encourage those involved. This counting of decisions for Christ is sometimes used to measure the success of a meeting or outreach event. Yet a year later where are these people? What happened to these spiritual infants? God has called His church to make disciples and the initial decision to follow Jesus as Lord is just the beginning.

Mass evangelism has been said to have the lowest retention rate where approximately 5-10% go on to become mature Christians. There may be several reasons for these observed low numbers, but one of the reasons is that the church has failed to disciple these spiritual babies. Individuals within the church did not effectively reach out to build relationships with them so that these new believers could be discipled and eventually grow into mature Christians. In many cases, a new believer may be given a Bible, a pamphlet or handout, instructed to read and pray, and then told to come back to church service the next week with no additional communication in between. When and if the new believer returns to church, they might find people who are friendly and who will engage them in conversation while at church. The number of those individuals who may be interested in the new believer enough to get to know them, or even make a phone call is often few.

It is important to remember that new believers have plenty of non-Christian friends when making a decision to receive and follow Jesus. If these new believers don't find new friendships within the body of Christ, they may find themselves spending a lot of time with their non-Christian friends. The non-Christian friends don't understand the decision the new believer has made to follow Christ and therefore have the potential to negatively influence that person and pull them away from the things of God. When the church family does not make the new believer feel like a part of the family, they often feel more comfortable with their unsaved friends. If the church does not gather the harvest of souls and invest in their lives, someone else or some other group will.

New believers must be nurtured and cell ministry provides a means for nurturing and training them. If the new believer is birthed into the Kingdom of God outside of the church service setting, such as at an outreach event, the person may be more comfortable with attending the cell group as a first step before attending the church service. What could be a next step if the new believer is hesitant to attend a cell group or even come to a church service? The individual that led them to Christ can continue to work on building a relationship and allowing them to get to the point of feeling comfortable enough to take additional steps forward. It is recommended in these cases that the soul-winner or discipler set up appointments with the new believer for times of sharing, bible study and prayer. Regular contact on a one-on-one basis is important, at least weekly in person if possible, in addition to regular phone contact. When the discipler is consistent, then trust is established and the new believer is often ready to make additional steps toward joining the cell group, being connected to the local church family and planted in the church.

For those new believers that come into cell groups immediately upon salvation, each cell group member may play some part in discipling and encouraging that person either directly or indirectly; although a key individual should be assigned to ensure that the new believer connects or builds a relationship with at least one person.

THE DISCIPLE OF CHRIST

A disciple is a pupil of Jesus, a follower of Christ and His teachings. The word "disciple" is mentioned in 27 verses in the New Testament. It was understood in biblical times that if an individual repented of sins, and confessed Jesus to be both Lord and Savior, they would be instructed in Christ's doctrine and become a follower or disciple of

Jesus. This new disciple would be encouraged to submit to being instructed by his teacher(s) willingly. If an individual is sincere in their decision to receive Jesus as Lord, they will be willing to be instructed in God's word. When the sinner is translated from the kingdom of darkness through salvation into God's Kingdom, it is an entirely new world for them (Colossians 1:13, II Corinthians 5:17). God's Kingdom operates on an entirely different set of principles from the kingdom of darkness. The new believer needs to be renewed in their way of thinking and this is a process (Romans 12:2). They must come to understand God's word and His ways and learn to apply the word to their lifestyle. God has called the church and the individuals within the church, to teach the new believer to observe the word of God. Teaching them extends beyond church services. Relationship must be established and mature Christians must lead and teach by example (II Corinthians 3:2). Once the new believer has grown to learn to observe the word of God in their everyday living, they then transition to a mature Christian; a disciple.

> *Matthew 28:19-20, "Go ye therefore, and teach all nations, baptizing them in the name of the Father, and of the Son, and of the Holy Ghost: Teaching them to observe all things whatsoever I have commanded you: and, lo, I am with you always, even unto the end of the world. Amen."*

PREPARING TO BE ONE WHO DISCIPLES OTHERS

Discipling new believers requires sacrifice, love and patience. In being one who disciples others, remember that God was longsuffering and patience with us as we had to "work out our own soul salvation" and He continues to be patient (Philippians 2:12). When it comes to sacrifice, often the biggest sacrifice is TIME. Investing in the lives of individuals requires time and sacrifice. Since everyone seems to be busy in this fast paced new millennium time we live in, who is really excluded from investing in the lives of new believers? For the Christian, sacrifice is our "reasonable service" and a part of living for Jesus. If we sincerely seek God concerning our time (daily or weekly schedules), He can show us how we can make adjustments in order to build His people through discipleship.

> *Romans 12:1, "I beseech you therefore, brethren, by the mercies of God, that ye present your bodies a living sacrifice, holy, acceptable unto God, which is your reasonable service."*

New believers often have no idea what it means to be a Christian in terms of lifestyle. They start off learning a few scriptures and often pattern themselves after others they believe are true Christians and who know the Bible. Although we must always instruct new believers to pattern themselves after Jesus Christ, they are just learning who Jesus is according to scripture and through personal relationship with Him. They may not fully know the nature and pattern of Jesus. Therefore, it is important to remember to lead by biblical example so that the new believer can learn not only from what they are taught in the word but also from what they are shown. Holiness and Christian character must be evident in the lives of those who will disciple others. It is one thing to tell a new believer how to seek God, but an entirely different thing to show them.

> *II Thessalonians 3:7-9, "For yourselves know how ye ought to follow us: for we behaved not ourselves disorderly among you...Not because we have not power, but to make ourselves an ensample unto you to follow us."*

Conclusion

Cell group ministry within the local church can be an effective means of providing an avenue to build closer relationships among members, provide for pastoral care and accountability, teaching and training, as well as development of mature Christians. Since cell group ministry can often lean toward being inward focused exclusively, a plan must be established to ensure the need to be outward focused is not overlooked and evangelistic strategies are implemented. The growth and expansion of cell groups means the growth and expansion of the local church. God has called us to make disciples and as evangelism is emphasized as a core value of the cell group, as well as prayer, worship, teaching and edification, there will be multiplication and expansion.

REFLECTION

1. Prior to reading this chapter, what was your understanding of cell group ministry as it relates to evangelism? In what way has your understanding changed since reading this chapter?

2. What can the cell group do in order to not become so inwardly focused that the outward focus is being omitted?

3. What is friendship evangelism as it relates to this chapter?

4. Provide some examples of ways the church or cell group can reach out to the community to show love and build relationships based on this chapter? What can your local church or cell group do?

SECTION II

Foundations in Evangelism –
Equipping for Kingdom Harvest

-Six-
MAKE DISCIPLES OF ALL NATIONS

FOUNDATION
Matthew 28:19, "Go therefore and make disciples of all the nations, baptizing them in the name of the Father and of the Son and of the Holy Spirit." (New King James Version)

From the very beginning God has purposed for those created in His likeness and in His image, for those who have His spirit, to have dominion. Adam and Eve were given dominion over the earth and became God's delegated authority. Genesis 1:28 says, "And God blessed them, and God said unto them, Be fruitful, and multiply, and replenish the earth, and subdue it: and have dominion over the fish of the sea, and over the fowl of the air, and over every living thing that moveth upon the earth." Although Adam sinned and lost his place of dominion and rule, through Jesus Christ many were made righteous and restored into a rightful place with God with restored authority (Romans 5:19).

The establishment of God's Kingdom rule is the plan and will of God. When the disciples asked Jesus how to pray, He told them to pray "Thy Kingdom come, Thy will be done in earth, as it is in heaven" (Matthew 6:10). As the sinner repents, receives the forgiveness of God, and receives the Holy Spirit, they are called to submit to Jesus and come under His Kingdom rule. They must learn the culture or lifestyle of God's Kingdom and become established in His word. Then they are to be equipped and sent to share the gospel of the Kingdom and bear fruit that remains (John 15:16). This process, when repeated again and again, causes souls to be added to the Kingdom and brings Kingdom expansion.

Some of us in certain Christian circles hear messages on Kingdom dominion in sermons, conferences or workshops that speak of dominion through Kingdom financing, dominion in the marketplace, dominion through land ownership and real estate, exercising spiritual dominion through strategic prayer and other areas where the church should exercise dominion. While we learn to exercise dominion in many key areas as a church, we cannot neglect focusing on Kingdom dominion through the "making of disciples." As more and more disciples are developed who have a commitment to the gospel and know how to exercise their God given authority, advancement of the Kingdom occurs more rapidly as the nations become disciples of our Lord Jesus Christ. The number of disciples can and will multiply greatly as the church commits to the winning of souls and discipleship.

> *Acts 6:7, "And the word of God increased; and the number of the disciples multiplied in Jerusalem greatly; and a great company of the priests were obedient to the faith."*

There have been many churches in America that have seen decreased church growth and expansion for various reasons. Some churches have grown, but not all have grown due to the unsaved becoming believers, but by believers transferring from one church to another. True church growth will be realized as more churches are committed to winning souls and making disciples.

GETTING DECISIONS VERSUS MAKING DISCIPLES

Are we making disciples or getting decisions for Christ? Are we getting people to make a verbal decision to accept Jesus and His forgiveness then praying with them, or are we leading people into discipleship as they make a commitment to *follow* Jesus? Some might wonder, "What's the difference?" The difference is major.

When the unsaved respond to an invitation to accept Jesus, in the mind of some that means, "I believe in Jesus, I agree that I need Him, and I know that I should ask for forgiveness." The person may believe in the word of God, may believe they need God, and then come forward acknowledging that need. Acknowledgement is a good first step, but this first step should lead to the next step of *true* repentance and a willingness to follow Jesus as Lord in order to be a disciple.

> *II Corinthians 7:9-10, "Now I rejoice, not that ye were made sorry, but that ye sorrowed to repentance: for ye were made sorry after a godly manner, that ye might receive damage by us in nothing. For godly sorrow worketh repentance to salvation not to be repented of: but the sorrow of the world worketh death."*

The above scripture tells us that there are two types of sorrow. Verse 10 speaks of a godly sorrow that produces the fruit of repentance that leads to salvation. Verse 10 also speaks of a worldly sorrow that produces no fruit. If an individual does not have godly sorrow that leads to repentance, the fruit of leading a person through the sinner's prayer will not produce the fruit of salvation and the evidence of a transformed life.

> *II Corinthians 5:17, "Therefore if any man be in Christ, he is a new creature: old things are passed away; behold, all things are become new."*

We may not know at first, except by discernment, whether a person has truly repented of sin with a godly sorrow and is willing to follow Jesus, but this is where prayer and follow-up ministry becomes very important. Through follow-up ministry (calling or speaking to the individual, setting up times for prayer and teaching, etc.) we learn whether the person truly has a desire to change and shows evidence of a commitment. We may also learn whether they made a decision to accept Jesus while not being sure of making a full commitment to follow Jesus.

During follow-up ministry, a person can go from being unsure of a commitment to Christ to a full commitment to follow Christ, so it's important to not be discouraged and follow through with the individual. Additional prayer and teaching, as the Spirit of the Lord deals with the individual, can lead to seeing the fruit of true repentance.

There can be times during follow-up ministry where the person who made a decision for Christ is not responsive to phone calls, seem disinterested, and shows no desire to connect with you or other believers. In these instances, it is best to pray about whether to continue to reach out to them and pray for their full commitment to Jesus. It's important to remember that we are in a spiritual battle and the enemy does not want that person to truly surrender to Christ. The church must be committed to warring in the spirit through prayer for the souls of men.

During follow-up ministry we will also find those who have truly made a decision to follow Jesus with their whole heart and show the evidence of that commitment. These individuals need to be properly discipled so that they may grow into a mature disciple who can in turn lead others to Christ.

> *Matthew 28:19, "Go therefore and make disciples of all the nations, baptizing them in the name of the Father and of the Son and of the Holy Spirit." (New King James Version)*

Jesus has called His church to make disciples of all nations. So those who have truly made a decision to follow Him, responding to His love with godly sorrow and repentance, need to not be left alone to figure out how to live for Christ. New believers who have been birthed into the Kingdom, translated from darkness to light, need nurturing, prayer, teaching and support. Even as a new baby in the natural needs proper care and nourishment for healthy and strong development, new babes in Christ are not to be left alone to figure out how to feed themselves (spiritually) or left unclothed with no prayer covering.

THE NEW CONVERT

> *James 5:19-20, "Brethren, if any of you do err from the truth, and one convert him; Let him know, that He which converteth the sinner from the error of His way shall save a soul from death, and shall hide a multitude of sins."*

In a biblical sense, a new convert is a person who has made a choice in response to the drawing and conviction of the Holy Spirit to change the error of his way, believe on the truth of the gospel, repent with godly sorrow and receive forgiveness. This person has chosen to follow Jesus and turn from his own way. In response to sincere repentance, the Holy Spirit comes to dwell within the individual and hence they are born again and are a new creature in Christ (John 3:3, II Corinthians 5:17). Although they have made a decision to submit to God, they may not know how to do this, and may know very little of the word of God. They will face various situations where they are challenged to live according to their old way of life. Although the Holy Spirit can lead them and will lead them as they cry out to God for help and direction, God has ordained that new converts be discipled. Multiple statements, as you've read, stressing the need to disciple new converts cannot be over emphasized when considering the lack of attention given to discipleship in many churches today.

THE DISCIPLE OF JESUS CHRIST

The disciple of Jesus Christ is one who has devoted himself to following Jesus and His teachings. One cannot truly follow Jesus in complete loyalty and allegiance without following His word, since Jesus is the word manifested (John 1:1). Through the making of disciples, mature believers are developed as the new disciple comes to understand Lordship, obedience, and God's unconditional love.

The Bible tells us that the disciples of Jesus Christ were first called Christians in Antioch (Acts 11:26). They were recognized as followers of Jesus Christ and His teachings. In short biblical definition, a Christian is a disciple, and a disciple is a follower of Jesus. Many people today who identify themselves as Christians, yet are not disciples (followers of Christ and His teachings), do so because they lack understanding of what it means to be a Christian.

As the church seeks to obey the gospel mandate to preach

the gospel to the ends of the earth, the preaching must include "making disciples" and helping new converts understand what becoming a disciple really means. The church must teach new converts that if they want to identify themselves as a Christian, this means choosing to become Christ's disciple and submitting to His Lordship.

As the early church expanded, the apostles understood they were to make disciples. Unfortunately today, the church has placed more emphasis on getting decisions for Christ with minimal follow-up versus seeing new believers become true disciples through a commitment to disciple them. Preaching the gospel and making disciples go hand in hand for it is the mandate of God.

BECOMING THE DISCIPLE OF CHRIST
Becoming a true disciple of Christ is the next step after the initial point of decision and conversion. Through conversion the new convert receives the Holy Spirit which enables them to walk free from sin. Following the conversion the individual must be willing to make a conscious daily decision to be submitted to God in ALL things, allowing God to bring change to ALL areas of his life. This is most certainly a process and God makes His grace available to the new believer (II Corinthians 12:9-10).

Jesus requires that we love Him with ALL of our heart, mind, soul and strength (Mark 12:30). Loving God any less than ALL is not acceptable with Him. Becoming Christ's disciple requires our ALL of EVERYTHING. Transitioning from a decision for Christ, to new convert, to truly becoming Christ's disciple is a process as the Holy Spirit moves on the heart of the individual. Each victory and act of submission leads to the next victory, and the daily decision to follow Christ allows the Holy Spirit to move within the heart and mind of the new believer.

Sometimes for fear of losing the new believer, offending him, or appearing "too hard" the new believer may not be challenged in the spirit of love and grace to truly become Christ's disciple, submit to Lordship, and make lifestyle changes. This fear of not offending has contributed to the modern day watered down version of what it means to be Christian. Jesus was not concerned about offending those that decided they wanted to follow Him. After some of His disciples heard a hard saying they chose to no longer walk with Him and then others stayed (John 6:63-66). Jesus made it clear that following Him meant giving up everything they had, yielding all of their life, to receive new life in Christ.

THE DISCIPLE OF CHRIST MUST LOVE JESUS MORE THAN POSSESSIONS

Jesus invited the rich man to follow Him but once he was challenged to give up everything, he chose not to be Christ's disciple. Jesus knew what was in his heart. In order for the new believer to become Christ's disciple he must be willing to let go of whatever Christ commands (Luke 14:33).

> *Matthew 19:21-22, "Jesus said unto him, If thou wilt be perfect, go and sell that thou hast, and give to the poor, and thou shalt have treasure in heaven: and come and follow me. But when the young man heard that saying, he went away sorrowful: for he had great possessions."*

THE DISCIPLE OF CHRIST MUST GIVE HIMSELF TO THE PRIORITIES OF JESUS

In order to be a disciple of Christ, God's priorities must have precedence in our lives. When Jesus calls us to follow Him, He demands that we come without delay.

> *Matthew 8:20-22, "And Jesus saith unto him, The foxes have holes, and the birds of the air have nests; but the Son of man hath not where to lay His head. And another of His disciples said unto him, Lord, suffer me first to go and bury my father. But Jesus said unto him, Follow me; and let the dead bury their dead."*
>
> *Matthew 8:20-22, "And Jesus replied to him, Foxes have holes and the birds of the air have lodging places, but the Son of Man has nowhere to lay His head. Another of the disciples said to Him, Lord, let me first go and bury [care for till death] my father. But Jesus said to him, Follow Me, and leave the dead [in sin] to bury their own dead." (Amplified Version)*

In the case of the disciple noted here in scripture, this man was already Christ's disciple but decided that he had something more important to do. Jesus was not being insensitive to this particular disciple, as his father was not dead. As supporting evidence for this has been noted in some commentaries providing biblical background on the above scriptures, this man's father must have been near the end of his years (an elderly man) and the disciple wanted to go away then return again after the eventual death and burial of his father. How long would it have been before the eventual death of his father particularly if he was not ill? Could it have been years? One could only speculate.

There will always be things in life that require our attention and we can become consumed with the cares of this life. God is very mindful of the things that pertain to our lives because He loves us, but He has called His people to seek first the Kingdom (Matthew 6:33). Jesus has not commanded us to neglect important things or necessary things of life, but has called us to allow these things to have their proper place. God has called us to love even as God is love, and to love our families in particular, but not above loving Him. In order to be Christ's disciple we must be willing to continue to follow Him while not allowing distractions or the cares of this life to pull us away from Kingdom priorities.

THE DISCIPLE OF CHRIST MUST GIVE HIMSELF CONTINUALLY TO THE WORD OF GOD

John 8:31, "Then said Jesus to those Jews which believed on him, If ye continue in my word, then are ye my disciples indeed."

Abiding in the word of God is abiding in Jesus. Since a disciple is a follower of Christ and His teachings, a person cannot truly be a disciple without following in His teachings. A disciple cannot know the teachings of Jesus unless there is a continuance in the study and meditation of the word of God.

THE DISCIPLE OF CHRIST MUST ALLOW HIS RELATIONSHIP WITH JESUS TO HAVE PRIORITY OVER ALL OTHER RELATIONSHIPS

Luke 14:26, "If any man come to me, and hate not his father, and mother, and wife, and children, and brethren, and sisters, yea, and his own life also, he cannot be my disciple."

Luke 14:26, "If anyone comes to Me and does not hate his [own] father and mother [in the sense of indifference to or relative disregard for them in comparison with his attitude toward God] and [likewise] his wife and children and brothers and sisters–[yes] and even his own life also–he cannot be My disciple." (Amplified Version)

In the context of this scripture, of course Jesus is not calling us to literally hate our brother in order to follow Him, not in the sense of what we understand as hate. The Bible asks the question in I John 4:20, "how can we love God who we can't see but then hate our brother who we can see?" In Matthew 10:37-38, Jesus is telling us that the lives of our loved ones or our relationships with family, friends, or whomever cannot have priority in our heart over our relationship with Christ. We see from this same scripture that even our own lives or desires cannot have higher priority in order for us to be a disciple of Jesus. This is a tough saying but it is the word of God which does not change.

THE DISCIPLE OF CHRIST MUST BE FRUITFUL

John 15:8, "Herein is my Father glorified, that ye bear much fruit; so shall ye be my disciples."

Even as Adam was called to be fruitful and multiply, God has called His disciples to be fruitful. As the disciple of Christ continues in prayer and the word, it is God's desire that each disciple matures both naturally and spiritually and advances the Kingdom through doing the works of Jesus and making more disciples. Even as Jesus called the twelve disciples and gave them power to heal the sick and cast out demons, He delegated this same authority to His modern day disciples (Mark 16:17-18).

THE DISCIPLE OF CHRIST MUST GIVE HIS LIFE AS A SACRIFICE, DENYING HIMSELF, ALLOWING THE LIFE OF CHRIST TO LIVE THROUGH HIM

Matthew 16:24, "Then said Jesus unto his disciples, If any man will come after me, let him deny himself, and take up his cross, and follow me."

The Bible tells us to present our bodies as a living sacrifice and that this is our reasonable service, or the standard requirement (Romans 12:1). The disciple of Christ must sacrifice body, mind, life, and all.

THE DISCIPLE OF CHRIST MUST BE FAITHFUL

II Timothy 2:2, "And the things that thou hast heard of me among many witnesses, the same commit thou to faithful men, who shall be able to teach others also."

Timothy was exhorted by the Apostle Paul to commit the things of God to faithful men so that they in turn would teach others. There is an investment of much time, prayer, teaching and impartation in the making of disciples. God's desire is that those things which have been seeded or invested into the life of the new disciple would grow and produce fruit. New disciples are to be trained so that they may grow and mature but also be prepared to teach others. This is the principle of multiplication.

QUALIFICATIONS FOR THE DISCIPLER

Philippians 4:9, "Those things, which ye have both learned, and received, and heard, and seen in me, do: and the God of peace shall be with you."

As we examine Philippians 4:9, we see that Paul is admonishing the people of God to follow the model he has demonstrated before them. They were admonished to take note of the things:

- Learned
- Received
- Heard
- Seen

The one who disciples must remember that a new convert who has committed to discipleship is not only learning from being instructed in the word of God, but is learning by what he or she sees demonstrated in the life of the mature believer. Just as a small child learns directly from being taught and instructed, there is much learning that comes indirectly through observation. So then the disciple, (the teacher, or more mature believer) must teach, impart, counsel, admonish and model a Kingdom lifestyle before the one being discipled. God has commanded that we make disciples, but we must be careful how we reproduce. The one who disciples is not required to have zero imperfections, or else no one would be qualified, but are called to walk in sound Christian character and have a good foundation in the word of God.

Earlier in this chapter, we discussed some key points that are required to be a disciple of Jesus Christ. The one who disciples the new convert must himself be a disciple. The discipler cannot lead someone to a place where he's never been, so then he must demonstrate a life of sacrifice, self-denial, faithfulness, consistency in study of the word of God and in prayer, with a "seek first the Kingdom" commitment to Jesus. Just as the Holy Spirit moved in the life of Paul and caused him to present a model of the disciple of Christ before the people, the Spirit of God works within all of our lives to enable us to be and do those things we could not otherwise accomplish in our own strength.

THE DISCIPLESHIP PROCESS

It's important for those that will disciple others to remember that the new convert has entered into a new Kingdom, must learn a new lifestyle, a new way of thinking, a new way of responding to life's challenges, develop new Christian relationships, develop a prayer life, study life and the list goes on. Working with the new disciple requires lots of love, patience, and longsuffering, but can also be very rewarding as the disciple begins to grow and develop into a mature Christian.

In order to be most effective in being one that disciples others, it is important to follow the model Jesus has provided for us.

THE CALLING AND RESPONSE

Matthew 4:19, "And He saith unto them, Follow me, and I will make you fishers of men."

When Jesus called Peter and Andrew to be His disciples, they had a decision to make. They could drop everything they were doing to follow Jesus which involved sacrifice, denial and a decision to submit to Him as Master, or they could ignore the call and continue what they were doing. They chose to follow Jesus and submit to His authority.

Just as the disciples were called by Jesus and responded, there should be a mutual commitment between the new disciple and the discipler (the teacher, or more mature believer). The one who disciples must be prepared to commit himself to be the teacher, build relationship, and model Godly character. Then also the new disciple should be prepared to submit and be teachable as they have been called into the discipleship process not by man but by Jesus.

Although a mutual understanding between the discipler and new disciple is encouraged, it may not always be the best strategy in every instance to encourage such a formal arrangement and agreement. There may be times where a relationship begins through the follow up process and then gradually progresses without any formal discussion to become a "discipler – new disciple" relationship. Some new disciples may be in the process of working through issues of the heart and mind such as trust or commitment issues. These issues of trust may be due to past hurts or other life experiences, so insisting that they formally commit to discipleship may seem intimidating. The discipler will need to pray, get to know the new convert, and allow God to provide wisdom and direction as to how to work with them in the "disciple–new disciple" relationship.

Teaching The Word Of God

After Jesus taught the multitudes and shared parables, He often took time to further expound on the word of God secluded from the crowds so that He might answer the disciples' questions and provide clarity. It is important that the new disciple not only have scheduled times of instruction but be given opportunity to receive clarity as needed. The one who disciples must be willing to make himself available for times of instruction or even inopportune moments of teaching and discussion regarding the issues of life.

The new disciple needs to be established in key Christian foundations and come to understand the principles of the doctrine of Christ; repentance, salvation, faith, baptism, prayer amongst others (Hebrews 6:1-2).

TEACH AND DEMONSTRATE
A PRAYER AND WORSHIP LIFESTYLE

Matthew 6:9, "After this manner therefore pray ye: Our Father which art in heaven, Hallowed be thy name."

The disciples asked Jesus to teach them how to pray and He began instruction by giving them a prayer model. Within that prayer model there is worship and adoration, thanksgiving, declaration, petitions, repentance, forgiveness, prayer for direction and deliverance. The new disciple must come to understand these important elements of prayer and develop a hunger for not only the things pertaining to God, but for God Himself.

BUILDING RELATIONSHIP

Matthew 12:49, "And He stretched forth His hand toward His disciples, and said, Behold my mother and my brethren!"

Jesus spent three years with His disciples sharing the word of God, instructing by example, and even building relationship with them. He called them brothers. There can be varying degrees of relationship established between the discipler and the one being discipled. God can provide the insight and wisdom in how the relationship should be established. It is important to have a heart that is willing to build the type of relationship God wants to establish, and pour into the life of the one being discipled, even as Jesus poured into the lives of His disciples.

DEMONSTRATE, ACTIVATE AND RELEASE

Matthew 10:1, "And when He had called unto Him His twelve disciples, He gave them power against unclean spirits, to cast them out, and to heal all manner of sickness and all manner of disease."

The disciples walked closely with Jesus and saw Him heal the sick, cast out devils, raise the dead, and do numerous miracles. The Bible does not tell us that He gave specific instruction on *how* to do these things, but we do know from scripture that as miracles took place, the disciples were with Him observing. After Jesus determined the appropriate time of release, He gave them power (activated them) and sent them out (released them) to heal the sick and cast out devils (Matthew 10:1).

As the Holy Spirit determines the right time and season after much teaching and demonstration, it is important that the discipler begin to activate the new disciple in the gifts of God and release them to be a witness and do the works of Jesus. As the new disciple begins to see God use them to bless others, they are further encouraged to desire more of Jesus and more of His power at work in their lives.

PRAYER COVERING
Luke 22:32, "But I have prayed for thee, that thy faith fail not: and when thou art converted, strengthen thy brethren."

Jesus being fully aware of the plans of the enemy prayed for Peter that his faith would not fail. In John 17:9, we see Jesus praying for the disciples and all those who are to become disciples. God gives the discipler insight into the life of the new disciple and it's important that they are covered in prayer that they resist temptation and that their faith fail not.

DISCIPLESHIP POINTS TO AVOID
While there are several key points to remember in teaching a new disciple, this is a list of a few points to avoid in the

discipleship process.

CONDEMNATION
It is important to bring correction in the spirit of love and meekness, but being condemning or lacking in mercy is not the heart of the Father. The Holy Spirit convicts of sin but does not condemn. If the new disciple is in error, the discipler must bring correction in wisdom and pray that the Holy Spirit convicts of sin and gives true repentance to the new disciple.

TEACH PRINCIPLES AND NOT PERSONAL CONVICTIONS
It is important that the new disciple is taught biblical principles. It is important that the discipler know the difference between biblical principles and personal convictions. The new disciple may not be mature enough to know this difference. If personal convictions are shared then they should be prefaced as "my personal conviction is..." prior to sharing or instruction. Otherwise the new convert may take upon themselves the convictions of the discipler while not really understanding why they believe one way over another in regards to a particular matter or practice.

AVOID EXCLUSIVENESS
Although the new disciple may develop a good close relationship with the discipler, it is important that the discipler allows other God given relationships to develop with the new disciple. The new disciple should be encouraged to get involved in the community life of the local church. The discipler should not lay claim on the new disciple as "mine, mine, mine" nor should the new disciple expect to only be in relationship with the discipler exclusively. These conditions can develop into unhealthy relationships.

Avoid Control And Manipulation
Sometimes the new disciple, because of their love and respect for the discipler, may desire to be a blessing and may go the extra mile or two to do something special such as giving gifts or assistance. It is important that the discipler be sensitive and never take advantage of their kindness or vulnerability.

Emotional Dependency
God hates idolatry. Emotional dependency on the part of the new disciple can develop into idolatry. The discipler must be in the proper place within the heart and life of the new disciple. The discipler is to provide support, instruction and various forms of ministry to help the new disciple grow, but ultimately the new disciple must learn to look to Jesus for their needs. Just as a newborn develops into an older child and eventually learns how to do things on their own without so much help and assistance from the parent, the new disciple must be allowed to develop. The discipler must seek the wisdom of God on when and how to pull back and allow the new disciple to become more firmly established in their confidence in God.

Conclusion
The mandate of God is to preach the gospel of the Kingdom and make disciples of all nations. Until the church at large begins to "make disciples" again as in the days of the early church, our local assemblies may continue to have high percentages of believers who don't really grow and mature and are therefore incapable of being one used by God to make disciples of all nations. The failure to make disciples hinders Kingdom expansion and is contrary to the mandate given by Jesus Christ.

As mature believers begin to reexamine what the Bible says

about the disciple, begin to model these characteristics and bring clarity to its definition, believers will once again be challenged to become true disciples and then make disciples. As a commitment to discipleship is seen within the body of Christ, mature believers who disciple others will increase and the church will grow and advance with a greater momentum.

REFLECTION

1. According to John 15:16, why is Kingdom expansion important in the lives of each believer? How does it relate to discipleship? Give two scripture references.

2. Based on this chapter, if you are a follower of Jesus Christ and his teachings you are a disciple. True or False (Circle one)

3. Which should come first in a new believer's life, discipleship or conversion?

4. When reviewing the section "Qualifications for the Discipler" in this chapter, what were the four specific things that the Apostle Paul admonished the Philippians to note?

5. Explain your own personal goals for discipleship. After reading this chapter, have you experienced a greater sense of urgency as it relates to training others and encouraging new believers to develop a committed relationship as true disciples of Christ?

-Seven-
COMPASSION MINISTRY
THE FATHER'S LOVE THROUGH DEMONSTRATION

FOUNDATION

Psalms 86:15, "But thou, O Lord, art a God full of compassion, and gracious, long-suffering, and plenteous in mercy and truth."

The love of God is not like the love of the world but is supernatural and supersedes any degree of love demonstrated by this world. The love of the world, the soulish kind of love, can be conditional and selfish at times but the love of God is always unconditional and selfless. The Bible tells us in John 15:13 "Greater love has no man than this, that a man lay down his life for his friends."

Jesus commissioned the church to go into all the world and preach the gospel of the Kingdom, and this Kingdom message includes salvation, deliverance, healing, provision, protection and so much more. Even as our God is love, and full of compassion, so has He called His people to be in this world (I John 4:16-17). The body of Christ has not only been called to preach the gospel in word only, but to reflect who He is to the world; a God of mercy, love, and compassion. Through acts of love and compassion, the world can see the love of the Father through His people in a tangible way as the sick are healed, the broken hearted are comforted, the hungry are fed, the naked are clothed, and the homeless are sheltered.

In this chapter we will examine scriptures that reveal the Father's compassionate heart regarding the poor while examining the various avenues by which the church may show forth the love and compassion of God as a part of a Kingdom lifestyle.

PITY VERSUS COMPASSION

Is it possible to have pity for someone and not be moved with compassion? Let's examine the definitions for the two words pity and compassion.

Pity: sympathetic sorrow for one suffering, distressed, or unhappy.[1]

Compassion: sympathetic consciousness of others' distress together with a desire to alleviate it.[2]

As we read these definitions we see that pity is a sympathetic emotion (a feeling) that may or may not lead to action, while compassion implies both pity and a sympathetic emotion coupled with an urgent desire to act and meet a need.

> *I Peter 3:8, "Finally, be ye all of one mind, having compassion one of another, love as brethren, be pitiful, be courteous."*

COMPELLED TO MINISTER

To be compelled means "to be driven by a forceful or strong urge."[3] Jesus was compelled to minister. He was moved by a great love and compassion to minister to those in need. His ministry to those that were hungry, lepers, blind or taken captive by demons was more than an act of obedience to the Father, but a compelling act of love and compassion.

> *Matthew 14:14, "And Jesus went forth, and saw a*

> *great multitude, and was moved with compassion toward them, and He healed their sick."*
>
> *Matthew 15:32, "Then Jesus called His disciples unto Him, and said, I have compassion on the multitude, because they continue with Me now three days, and have nothing to eat: and I will not send them away fasting, lest they faint in the way."*
>
> *Matthew 20:34, "So Jesus had compassion on them, and touched their eyes: and immediately their eyes received sight, and they followed him."*
>
> *Mark 1:41, "And Jesus, moved with compassion, put forth His hand, and touched him, and saith unto him, I will; be thou clean."*

In order to fulfill all the Lord has commissioned the church to do, we must not only have a heart of obedience, but a heart of compassion that compels us to move and act motivated by love. Otherwise, our ministry and acts of kindness and charity may simply be motivated out of seeking justification through works, a religious obligation, or even a desire to appear pious before the people.

> *I Corinthians 13:3, "And though I bestow all my goods to feed the poor, and though I give my body to be burned, but have not love, it profits me nothing." (New King James Version)*

THE POOR AND NEEDY: A HEAVENLY PERSPECTIVE

As it has been for many ages, the poor and the destitute, the orphaned, the lame and diseased, have often been despised by the world and even looked upon as a burden. In the streets of many urban cities live the homeless, the destitute, those that have lost hope and live in a world within a world who for the most part has not regarded them as a relevant part of the community. The Father's love for them, His destiny and desire for them, is not any less than that for the privileged. To the contrary, His desire is to raise them up as a praise in the earth to show forth His glory and power for all the world to see.

> *I Samuel 2:7-9, "The LORD maketh poor, and maketh rich: He bringeth low, and lifteth up. He raiseth up the poor out of the dust, and lifteth up the beggar from the dunghill, to set them among princes, and to make them inherit the throne of glory: for the pillars of the earth are the LORD's, and He hath set the world upon them. He will keep the feet of His saints, and the wicked shall be silent in darkness; for by strength shall no man prevail."*

The people of God must look at the poor, the hurting, the homeless and the needy through the eyes of Jesus and through the eyes of love, for it very well may be that the teenager lying in the street from a drug overdose is destined to be the next great world leader. All things are possible with God (Matthew 19:26).

(Additional verses: Psalms 72:12-14, Isaiah 58:6-8, Luke 4:18-19, Leviticus 23:22)

ALIGNING OUR HEARTS WITH JESUS

Living in a world where the hearts of so many people have been given to their own devices, self-gain, self-promotion and personal fulfillment, it is important that the heart of God's servants is totally given to Him. For if our hearts are not totally given to Jesus continually, then our desires will not be fully aligned with God's purposes. We then risk having a heart that has "waxed cold" with a lukewarm love (Revelation 3:16). Instead of reflecting the love of Jesus, we begin to look and respond like the world.

> *Matthew 24:12, "And because iniquity shall abound, the love of many shall wax cold."*
>
> *I John 3:17, "But whoso hath this world's good, and seeth his brother have need, and shutteth up his bowels of compassion from him, how dwelleth the love of God in him?"*

In the following scripture, we see a word of correction came to the church as the poor were despised and the rich highly regarded. This is not the heart of the Father.

> *James 2:5-7, "Hearken, my beloved brethren, Hath not God chosen the poor of this world rich in faith, and heirs of the kingdom which He hath promised to them that love him? But ye have despised the poor. Do not rich men oppress you, and draw you before the judgment seats? Do not they blaspheme that worthy name by the which ye are called?"*

The Lord commands us to not stop our ears at the cries of the poor nor hide our eyes.

> *Proverbs 21:13, "Whoso stoppeth his ears at the cry of the poor, he also shall cry himself, but shall not be heard."*
>
> *Proverbs 28:27, "He that giveth unto the poor shall not lack: but he that hideth his eyes shall have many a curse."*

If we find that our love has grown lukewarm or that we, like many in the world, have despised the poor and considered them a burden, we must repent and allow the Lord to bring revival in our hearts. As we cry out to Him with a contrite heart, He will renew us again, and cause our hearts to be renewed with the fullness of His love that we may be His instruments of love and deliverance (Isaiah 57:15).

THE PROMISE OF BLESSING

Not only has the Lord chosen us to preach the gospel and to reflect His love and compassion to the world, He has also promised blessings as we minister to the poor.

> *Psalms 41:1-2, "Blessed is he that considereth the poor: the LORD will deliver him in time of trouble. The LORD will preserve him, and keep him alive; and he shall be blessed upon the earth: and thou wilt not deliver him unto the will of his enemies."*

> *Luke 14:12-14, "Then said he also to him that bade him, When thou makest a dinner or a supper, call not thy friends, nor thy brethren, neither thy kinsmen, nor thy rich neighbours; lest they also bid thee again, and a recompense be made thee. But when thou makest a feast, call the poor, the maimed, the lame, the blind: And thou shalt be blessed; for they cannot recompense thee: for thou shalt be recompensed at the resurrection of the just."*

As we feed the hungry, give water to the thirsty, clothe the naked, visit the sick and those in prison, Jesus said when we minister to the least of these we in turn minister to Him (Matthew 25:34-40). For in doing this Jesus calls us blessed and has promised an inheritance.

TO GIVE OR NOT TO GIVE?

The world population is now approximately seven billion people. Half of which has never heard the gospel and half of which live on less than three dollars per day. Let's take a look at some facts.[4]

- About half the world - over three billion people - live on less than $2.50 per day.
- At least 80% of humanity lives on less than $10 a day.
- According to UNICEF, 22,000 children die each day due to poverty. And they "die quietly in some of the poorest villages on earth, far removed from the scrutiny and the conscience of the world. Being meek and weak in life makes these dying multitudes even more invisible in death."
- Number of children in the world: 2.2 billion.
- Number in poverty: 1 billion (every second child).

With these kind of statistics, one can almost feel overwhelmed when desiring to make a difference in the lives of people. God has not called us to meet every need in every place, but as we seek His direction concerning our giving and our serving, He has promised to direct us (Proverbs 3:6). When we are led by the Holy Spirit, and seek to know His will and obey His voice, we will know in which ways we can be a blessing and it will not be a burden to us. The Lord has told us that His yoke is easy and His burden is light (Matthew 11:30). He will direct us in which times, instances, and places we are to give and when not to give.

In urban areas where there may be an abundance of beggars, or in instances where begging has become a self-imposed occupation for some, it becomes even more important to know the voice of God and how to respond. These almost weekly encounters in some cases can seem like a nuisance and it's important that we guard our hearts. If we really want to know the heart of the Father concerning each individual, He will reveal it to us. The key is being open to hear God's voice out of a caring heart. God reigns on the just and the unjust, so we must not always dismiss or write off the hustler or professional beggar. God may give us a life changing word for a particular individual as He directs us to give a cup of coffee, a cold beverage, or even bless them monetarily. It is the goodness of the Lord that leads sinners to repentance, and the encounter they have with one of His servants may be a life changing one (Romans 2:4).

BLESSED TO BE A BLESSING: REACHING OUT TO INDIVIDUALS AND COMMUNITIES

Even as Abraham was called to be blessed and to be a blessing, we the spiritual descendants of Abraham are called to be a blessing to the nations (Genesis 12:2). As we obey the apostolic mandate to preach the gospel and look for God given opportunities to reach the lost, we should also allow God to show us how we may be a blessing in our everyday living. Demonstrating acts of compassion and showing forth God's love must become a part of our lifestyle as Christians.

How can we bless the stranger, the homeless, the widow…? Perhaps we can provide something to eat to the homeless man when he has not requested anything from us at all? Maybe even offer to sit down and eat with him if time allows? Even with our busy lives and schedules there are ways. Perhaps we might be compelled to make a few care packages to keep in the car for distribution when directed by the Holy Spirit? These are just a few ideas.

WHAT CAN YOUR CHURCH DO?

Here are several ideas your church could use to reach your community:

- job training and employment resources
- adopting a public school with free tutoring provided
- child care service for single parents
- youth events and community sports programs
- community organizing to address neighborhood issues
- mentoring children of prisoners
- communicating the gospel through the arts
- programs to reduce recidivism
- door-to-door evangelism and home Bible studies
- various support groups addressing grief, addictions, etc.
- free legal counseling or services
- soup kitchen or food pantry
- health, fitness and nutrition resources
- financial counseling and workshops
- senior advocacy and support services
- advocacy for abused women and children
- family counseling and parenting seminars
- conflict resolution training and mediation
- car repair service for low-income families
- summer community outreach events for families

- GED classes, ESL training
- shelter or transitional housing for homeless persons
- community beautification projects

More and more ideas will be generated as you assess the needs of your community and seek the Lord for guidance and strategy.

DISASTER RELIEF

Times of crisis and natural disasters (hurricanes, earthquakes, tornados, etc.) are critical times of need where the church can minister to both the physical and spiritual needs of those affected. There are training programs available across the country to help individuals and organizations be more prepared to provide relief during crisis.[5] Secular organizations do a tremendous job at meeting the physical needs of people during crisis but are not prepared to meet the spiritual needs of those shaken by trauma, fear and hopelessness. If we, the church, make ourselves more available, additional churches and faith based organizations can be trained and mobilized for mass relief efforts.

CONCLUSION

The word of God tells us to love the Lord our God with ALL our heart, ALL our mind, and ALL our soul and strength and then love our neighbor as ourselves (Mark 12:29-31). In fulfilling this New Testament commandment we in turn fulfill the mandate of God to reach the world with the gospel and reflect the love of Christ in deed and charity.

It is clearly evident from scripture that charity and giving to the poor are to be a part of the lifestyle for God's people. As the apostles were commending Paul and Barnabas to their ministry to the Gentiles, they were instructed to be mindful of the poor (Galatians 2:10).

Let us be ever so mindful of the poor, both the naturally and the spiritually poor, and seek to be God's agents of love and compassion to the world. As we commit to this as Christians, may the poor come to know that Jesus loves them and desires to bring both provision and life transformation.

REFLECTION

1. Give four scripture references in which Jesus showed compassion to others based on the content of this chapter.

2. When was the last time the Father's love was shown through you to someone else in need? What did you do?

3. Has God placed someone on your heart to help? If yes, have you done so?

•

REFERENCE

1. *Merriam Webster Online Dictionary*, http://www.merriam.com
2. *Ibid*
3. *Ibid*
4. *Global Issues: Social, Political, Economic and Environmental Issues That Affect Us All. Causes of Poverty*, Website: http://www.globalissues.org
5. Dr. Denny and Sandy Nissley, certified in Individual Crisis Intervention, hosts Faith Based First Responders Conferences. For more information go to: http://www.christinaction.com/index.cfm/PageID/10/index.html

-Eight-
STRATEGIC PRAYER AND EVANGELISM

FOUNDATION

Prayer that is consistent and strategic is vitally important in the work of evangelism ministry. George Barna, author of Evangelism That Works[1] says, "A church that strives to evangelize its community without saturating its efforts in prayer is like a race car driver that jumps into a car at the starting line and discovers that the tank has not been filled with gas."

A short definition of Strategic Prayer and Evangelism is "intentional, Spirit led prayer coupled with Spirit directed evangelism that yields a great harvest of fruit that remains." The fruit is the souls of men. To be intentional in evangelism means the action is taken by intent or design. There are times when the unction to pray arises and the time of intercession is unplanned, but we must PLAN to PRAY and allow God to lead us in that plan. Evangelism, as well as prayer, must be intentional and done in partnership with the Holy Spirit.

Prayer for evangelism is biblical[2] and Jesus instructed us in His word to pray for labourers to gather the harvest (Luke 10:2). There are times when we look at the world from a natural perspective and in doing so we may not see a harvest that is great and ripe, yet Jesus has called His people to open their spiritual eyes and see what He sees. John 4:35 says, "Do you not say, 'There are still four months and then comes the harvest'? Behold, I say to you, lift up your eyes and look at the fields, for they are already white for harvest!" (New King James Version) There was a ripe harvest then and there is a great harvest in our day. God has prepared the hearts of many who are at the threshold of coming into the Kingdom. We must pray for more labourers and for those souls in need of salvation.

Prayer is important in evangelism as it prepares the heart of the witness.[3] "Praying always with all prayer and supplication in the Spirit, and watching thereunto with all perseverance and supplication for all saints; *And for me, that utterance may be given unto me, that I may open my mouth boldly, to make known the mystery of the gospel*" (Ephesians 6:18-19). As we pray God prepares our hearts to be a bold witness for Him and to make known the mystery of the gospel.

Prayer in evangelism prepares the heart of the receiver[4] (II Corinthians 4:3-4). The Bible tells us that the gospel is hidden to those that are lost. The god (satan) of this world has blinded them. We must pray for their eyes to be opened and for the Holy Spirit to draw them. No man can come to God unless they are drawn by the Spirit of God. As we pray, God causes their eyes to be opened and the walls around their hearts that seemed impenetrable to be torn down.

We must pray and trust God to give us His heart for the lost and great grace to fulfill the apostolic mandate which is our commitment to the great commission (Matthew 28:19-20). God has called His church to make disciples of all nations. Each individual in the church must decide how they are going to respond to this mandate or commission given by God, whether in a loving heart of obedience or a heart of disobedience. Those with a heart of obedience will be willing to "pray" for the salvation of the nations while also being willing to "go" as the Lord leads.

> *Mark 16:15, "And He said unto them, Go ye into all the world, and preach the gospel to every creature."*

PRAYER FOUNDATIONS
Alignment of the Heart

In order for our hearts to be aligned or in agreement to what is on God's heart, we must allow Him to transform us in the place of prayer. In the place of prayer, in the midst of the presence and the glory of God, we are changed. In the place of prayer, God reveals His desires for our lives, for His church, and for those in need of salvation.

REMOVING BARRIERS TO INTIMACY WITH GOD

A barrier can be people, passions or things that we love more than God (Mark 12:30). We must allow God to help us remove these barriers in order to truly give ourselves to consistent, focused and committed prayer.

To love anything more than God is a barrier to drawing near to Him in prayer.

> *Matthew 10:37, "He that loveth father or mother more than me is not worthy of me: and he that loveth son or daughter more than me is not worthy of me."*

Sin is a barrier to intimacy with God. We cannot expect to dwell in the presence of God while practicing sin. God has called His people to confess and repent of sin and not willingly submit to and practice sin. According to Psalms 15:1-5, only those who walk upright and live righteously will dwell in God's Holy Hill; in the glory of God's presence. We must be willing to repent of sin and yield to righteousness to have a close relationship with God.

Isaiah 59:2, "But your iniquities have separated between you and your God, and your sins have hid His face from you, that He will not hear."

Pride, which is also sin, is a barrier to drawing near to God. If we desire to draw nearer to God we must be willing to remove pride out of our lives. The Bible tells us that God resists the proud but gives grace to the humble (I Peter 5:5). Posturing our hearts in a place of humility is required if we are to draw near to God and receive grace from Him.

At times we can become overwhelmed with the cares of this life, but if being overwhelmed becomes the norm this becomes a barrier to drawing near to God. In Luke 8:14, the parable of the seed and the sower, those who heard the word but became overwhelmed with the cares of life bore no fruit. In order for us to have a consistent, fruitful and effective prayer life we must allow God to order our steps and our lives in order to accomplish both spiritual and natural things. Being overwhelmed as the norm will hinder both prayer and spiritual growth in the life of the Christian.

Luke 21:34, "But take heed to yourselves and be on your guard, lest your hearts be overburdened and depressed (weighed down) with the giddiness and headache and nausea of self-indulgence, drunkenness, and worldly worries and cares pertaining to [the business of] this life, and [lest] that day come upon you suddenly like a trap or a noose." (Amplified Version)

EMBRACING A PRAYER LIFESTYLE
The scripture tells us in I Thessalonians 5:17 that God has called us to "Pray without ceasing." God has not called us

to intermittent, occasional prayer. For some Christians prayer has become communication with God that is based on specific needs at specific times instead of an ongoing communion with God out of a love relationship.

In order to embrace a prayer lifestyle there must be a willingness to submit to God and His priorities. The scripture tells us in Galatians 2:20, "I have been crucified with Christ; it is no longer I who live, but Christ lives in me; and the life which I now live in the flesh I live by faith in the Son of God, who loved me and gave Himself for me" (New King James Version). If we, the followers of Christ, truly embrace this scripture it means our former life (prior to salvation) is over and God has purposed for us to live unto Christ. Therefore our hearts must be willing to submit to not only personal prayer but those "prayer assignments" God gives us to pray through as intercessors. To be an intercessor means to be one who prays and petitions God on behalf of another. In evangelism ministry we are called to pray on behalf of the unsaved petitioning God for their salvation and deliverance.

If prayer is to be a priority in our lives and a part of our lifestyle we must be willing to die to our own desires and submit to God's Kingdom priorities. In doing so, it does not mean that we neglect the other important things that pertain to life. It is important that we learn to trust God to order our steps and believe by faith He will give us His wisdom and meet our needs.

> *Matthew 6:33, "But seek ye first the Kingdom of God, and His righteousness; and all these things shall be added to you." (New King James Version)*

A lifestyle of prayer for the believer is not an option but a command and calling. God has called us to obedience. If we call Him Lord, we must be willing to obey Him (Luke 6:46). If we are to follow Jesus as Lord of our lives, we must not only be willing to obey our calling to a prayer lifestyle but yield to the promptings of the Holy Spirit as He calls upon us to pray at specific times.

PURE HEART MOTIVES

It is important that we check our motives and periodically assess ourselves in reference to prayer. Do we pray in order to fulfill a spiritual obligation, out of ritual, or to "get something" from God only? God desires that we have pure motives that proceed from a pure heart when we come into that place of prayer which is communion with Him.

Matthew 5:8, "Blessed are the pure in heart; for they shall see God."

We see from the scripture in Psalms 51:10 the psalmist asks God to "Create in me a clean heart, O God; and renew a right spirit within me." This is something we should be willing to ask God to do for us regularly that He may purify our hearts and motives.

Deuteronomy 10:16, "Circumcise therefore the foreskin of your heart, and be no more stiffnecked."

God challenged His people to make a decision to allow their heart to be circumcised and to no longer be stubborn and resistant to the will of God. When we are to align our hearts with the purposes of God in prayer and His heart for the harvest, we must allow our hearts to be circumcised. Spiritual circumcision allows for the cutting away of that which is unrighteous in a spiritual sense. In doing this our prayers will be focused and motives pure.

POSTURE AND POSITION IN PRAYER

As believers we must remind ourselves that whether we are praying individual prayers or interceding for the lost, we are in partnership with the Holy Spirit and praying from a covenant position in God.

> *Hebrews 10:16, "This is the covenant that I will make with them after those days, saith the Lord, I will put my laws into their hearts, and in their minds will I write them."*

As disciples of Christ who are in covenant with God, we have privileges and promises as a result of that covenant, and we call our creator "Father" as we are His children.

> *Hebrews 10:22, "Let us draw near with a true heart in full assurance of faith, having our hearts sprinkled from an evil conscience, and our bodies washed with pure water."*

Having been forgiven of sin and cleansed, we can approach our Most Holy God with assurance and know that He receives us and hears our prayers and intercession.

> *Hebrews 4:16, "Let us therefore come boldly unto the throne of grace, that we may obtain mercy, and find grace to help in time of need."*

There are earthly protocols to approaching a king or royalty. A person seeking audience with a king would need to have permission first before approaching him. Our God and King has given His covenant people permission to come before His presence out of a relationship with Him and has called us to ask of Him in faith. God has extended His Holy scepter to us giving us special assess as believers. As we reverently come before the Lord in prayer, let us be reminded that He has opened the door and given us the privilege of close communion with Him.

> *Matthew 21:22, "And all things, whatsoever ye shall ask in prayer, believing, ye shall receive."*

Because we are in covenant with God, He chooses to reveal His plans with us and desires that we partner with Him through prayer (Amos 3:7).

God looks throughout the earth for those that will intercede and stand in the gap for individual souls, cities, and nations.

> *Ezekiel 22:30, "And I sought for a man among them, that should make up the hedge, and stand in the gap before me for the land, that I should not destroy it: but I found none."*

When God planned to destroy Sodom and Gomorrah, He chose to tell Abraham of His plans because of His covenant with him. Abraham began to intercede or stand in the gap for the cities but particularly for those righteous in the city (Genesis 18:17-33).

Because Abraham had covenant with God and was a friend of God, he realized he could petition the Lord from that covenant position or place of relationship.

UNDERSTANDING SONSHIP

Those who have received Jesus as Lord and Savior have been relationally positioned with God as a son or daughter in the Kingdom. Understanding what it means to be a son in relation to God helps us pray with a different posture and faith knowing that God honors our prayers.

John 1:12, "But as many as received Him, to them gave He power to become the sons of God, even to them that believe on His name."

Galatians 4:7, "Wherefore thou art no more a servant, but a son; and if a son, then an heir of God through Christ."

PRAYING WITH KINGDOM VISION
What is it that we see with our eyes in a spiritual sense? Do we envision a changed life as we pray for an unbeliever or do we only have hope while praying with little faith? Do we see a changed community as we pray for that community? God desires to reveal His heart and His vision for change to His intercessors so that those who pray will do so in alignment with a heavenly vision. God can prophetically cause us to see the transformation in the realm of the spirit before the transformation is actually revealed to the natural eyes. As we pray, we must pray with God inspired vision and not according to what we see in the natural realm. Praying with vision causes us to pray with faith. The Bible tells us in II Corinthians 5:7, "For we walk by faith, not by sight."

STRATEGIC INTERCESSION
What Makes Prayer Strategic?
First, let's define the word strategy. Strategy is a careful plan or, method; the art of devising or employing plans or stratagems toward a goal.[5]

Receiving God's Plan - Following God's Plan - Fulfillment of God's Will
God gives His plans or strategies in prayer for the purpose of seeing the fulfillment of His will as we, His church, pray according to His directives. God has not called us to just

pray only, but to pray according to His will and design. As we pray according to the word of God, while being led by the Spirit of God, we pray according to the will of God. It is important to study and know the word of God in order to pray in agreement with His will and purposes.

- Effectual fervent prayer (James 5:16)
- Prayer according to the scriptures (John 15:7)

THE ROLE OF THE HOLY SPIRIT IN STRATEGIC INTERCESSION

The Holy Spirit aids us in prayer as we are limited in our ability to intercede in our own strength and knowledge (Romans 8:26-27). As we yield to the Spirit of God in intercession we pray according to the will of God and not the will of man nor the will of the flesh. Being sensitive to the promptings of the Holy Spirit in prayer is key in praying strategically and in partnership with God.

UNDERSTANDING YOUR PRAYER ASSIGNMENT

Each of us within the Body of Christ have been given different gifts, have different strengths and have been given a different measure of grace (Romans 12:3-8). It is important that each of us minister according to the measure of grace we have been given and also pray according to the assignment or prayer focus we have received from God. There are so many things, individuals and regions to pray for when it comes to evangelism yet much can be done in the realm of the spirit when each person remains focused in their prayer assignment. It is important to remember that in order to be strategic in intercession we must be sensitive to God's Spirit and pray with purpose.

Faithfulness To A Prayer Assignment
Consistent And Sustained Prayer
God has called His servants to be faithful to that which He has called us to. In praying through the God given prayer assignment, one must be faithful and given to consistent prayer in order to see the results that God has intended. I Corinthians 4:1-2, "Let a man so account of us, as of the ministers of Christ, and stewards of the mysteries of God. Moreov'er it is required in stewards that a man be found faithful."

Overcoming Obstacles To Sustained Prayer
The section of this lesson on "Prayer Foundations" mentions several obstacles that can be a hindrance to intimacy with God. These obstacles can also in turn be a hindrance to sustained prayer. In addition to those obstacles or barriers listed in the section on "Prayer Foundations", another obstacle to sustained prayer in completing one's prayer assignment is "loss of focus." We must maintain our focus according to that which God has given and not try to multi-task, in a spiritual sense, to the extent that we are ineffective in praying for that which we have been given to pray for in a particular season.

Prayer And Spiritual Warfare
Discerning And Identifying
Demonic Opposition
II Corinthians 2:11 tells us that we are not ignorant of satan's devices. There have been wicked devices that the enemy has set in place to hinder the church from fulfilling the apostolic mandate. The enemy seeks to hinder a community, city or region from experiencing revival, and to hinder individuals from seeing their need for salvation. In order to develop an effective prayer plan or strategy it is

important that we confront demonic opposition in prayer as a part of that overall plan. As we seek God for direction, the Holy Spirit will show us what the demonic opposition is so that the opposition can be confronted in the realm of Spirit led prayer.

CONFRONTING DEMONIC OPPOSITION

Matthew 16:19, "And I will give unto thee the keys of the kingdom of heaven: and whatsoever thou shalt bind on earth shall be bound in heaven: and whatsoever thou shalt loose on earth shall be loosed in heaven."

Matthew 16:19, "I will give you the keys of the kingdom of heaven; and whatever you bind (declare to be improper and unlawful) on earth must be what is already bound in heaven; and whatever you loose (declare lawful) on earth must be what is already loosed in heaven." (Amplified Version)

There is much demonic activity that operates regularly while having limited confrontation with God's spiritual legislature, the CHURCH. When the church (local, national and global) is not consistent in Spirit led prayer, demonic spirits seek to establish or maintain strongholds. These strongholds affect that which we see in the natural realm. God has given His people authority to bind and loose and declare what can and cannot operate in the realm of the spirit. Through prayer we can declare that which is lawful and unlawful. Through prayer the church has been called to establish spiritual boundaries, to tear down demonic barriers, and to loose that which God desires to be released for His Kingdom purposes.

The word "Legislature" is defined as "an officially elected

or otherwise selected body of people vested with the responsibility and power to make laws for a political unit, such as a state or nation."[6] The church has been established in the earth by God with the responsibility to be a steward over the work of His hands, to declare that which is unlawful according to God's word, and to enforce spiritual laws through prayer.

SPIRIT LED ENGAGEMENT
Romans 8:14, "For as many as are led by the Spirit of God, they are the sons of God."

Although God has given His people authority and power to bind and loose, He also calls us to use wisdom in exercising that authority (Luke 10:19). The opposite of being led by the Spirit of God is being led by the flesh. As we pray and confront demonic opposition that hinders souls from entering the Kingdom let us pray with a heart of faith and humility, and from a position of Holy Spirit power and not in spiritual pride and reliance on our own efforts which is of the flesh.

PRAYER AND FASTING
What the Scriptures Say About Prayer and Fasting
Mark 9:27-29, "But Jesus took him by the hand, and lifted him up; and he arose. And when he was come into the house, His disciples asked him privately, Why could not we cast him out? And He said unto them, This kind can come forth by nothing, but by prayer and fasting." (emphasis added)

There are some demonic spirits that are more resistant than others and the scripture shows us that prayer coupled with fasting is necessary to confronting certain demonic opposition. Prayer with fasting releases renewed faith, a new grace, a new strength and power to break through.

THE FAST THAT GOD HAS CHOSEN - SPIRIT DIRECTED FASTING

Believers are called to live a lifestyle of prayer and fasting but there are certain times when the Lord will direct His people to fast and pray for specific things either individually or corporately; even prayer and fasting for souls. There is a fast that the Lord chooses and we must be sensitive to listen as He directs and obey with a heart of prayer and consecration (Isaiah 58:5).

OBSTACLES TO FASTING

Lack of prayer is an obstacle to fasting. If there is no discipline in the devotional life of the believer, then it can be difficult to be disciplined in ruling over the natural appetites in order to commit to times of fasting. Through consistent prayer the grace of God is released to fast in order that the fruit of fasting will be experienced and seen.

FASTING FOR REVIVAL

When an individual, church, city, or nation experiences revival, repentance with a desire for holiness, submission to God, and spiritual hunger are characteristic of this move of the Spirit.

God desires to revive, restore, and awaken His church. He does not awaken His church just so that the church can segregate themselves and stay behind the walls of a church building. He desires to use His people to pray for and reach out to the lost who are dead in their sins and in need of resurrection life. In order to see revival, those praying for revival will need to develop a spiritual hunger that exceeds natural hunger and produces a desire to pray and fast for spiritual breakthrough.

Prayer Walking

The purpose of prayer walking is to pray on location in order to get insight on what God desires to be main points of prayer focus. God will reveal things by the spirit as we seek His guidance while praying inside a building but even more can be revealed both naturally and spiritually as we pray on site. In addition, since all the land in the earth belongs to God, when we walk and pray we are declaring that truth and enforcing the dominion of God so that demonic kingdoms come into subjection to God's Kingdom rule.

Focus In Prayer Walking

- Pray according to what you KNOW[7] (general information)
- Pray according to what you SEE[8]
- Pray as the Holy Spirit INSPIRES[9]
- Pray according to what you've DISCOVERED (research)

When And Where To Prayer Walk

Prayer walking can be both scheduled and unscheduled. There may be instances when an individual or group is inspired by the Holy Spirit to prayer walk an area. Then there are other times when there is a desire to do a prayer walk as a result of having a concern or heart for a particular area.

Prayer walking can be effective when done as an individual or as a part of a team. God may lead an individual to pray for their neighborhood while out for a walk. God may lead a group or members of a congregation to pray for a community. Whichever way God directs us we must be obedient, faithful, and pray in faith.

We prayer walk targeted areas as they are revealed to us through prayer. Even as our military receives strategy from their commanders on how to engage the enemy in combat and where to infiltrate a territory, God gives specific directives to His army of believers of when and where in prayer walking. Be faithful to pray in the area or prayer target until God gives the directive to move or to engage the spiritual opposition with a different strategy.

EVANGELISM - REAPING THE HARVEST
Prayer Preparation and Evangelism Action
God empowers His people to be a witness for Him even as He empowered the first century church.

> *Acts 1:8, "But ye shall receive power, after that the Holy Ghost is come upon you: and ye shall be witnesses unto me both in Jerusalem, and in all Judaea, and in Samaria, and unto the uttermost part of the earth."*

We see from the scripture in the book of Acts that God has given His church power for purpose. That purpose is to be a witness. One can pray, and pray, and pray and bind the strongman but never take the initiative to reap the harvest. God has called us to pray but has also empowered His people to ACT; to witness.

Believers must pray for boldness when confronting the fear of witnessing in evangelism. When Peter and John were threatened not to preach in the name of Jesus, they gathered with the believers and prayed for boldness.

> *Acts 4:29-30, "And now, Lord, behold their threatenings: and grant unto thy servants, that with all boldness they may speak thy word, By stretching*

forth thine hand to heal; and that signs and wonders may be done by the name of thy holy child Jesus."

Prayer is vital to breaking through the barrier of fear that would hinder God's people from reaping the harvest.

EVANGELIZE!
BIND THE STRONG MAN AND TAKE THE SPOILS

Mark 3:27, "No man can enter into a strong man's house, and spoil his goods, except he will first bind the strong man; and then he will spoil his house."

The purpose of prayer as it relates to evangelism is to create a spiritual climate that is conducive to reaping a spiritual harvest. Through our intercession we bind the strong man (demonic spirits) that hinder salvation of individuals and hinder change in an area. Then we gather the spoil, the souls, as God prepares their hearts to receive the word of truth. Prayer is vital to evangelism and willing labourers are vital to reaping the harvest.

EXTENDING PRAYER TO THE UNSAVED

Prayer is a strategy that has been used to engage the heart of the unbeliever. As the believer extends prayer, and the unbeliever agrees to receive prayer, God uses this encounter to deal with the heart of the unbeliever and bring receptiveness and a greater degree of openness to receive the word of God. The Holy Spirit may lead you to extend prayer in many different instances and in various settings that God may bring a swift answer to prayer, show His love and mercy, and give men repentance (Romans 2:4).

STRATEGIC EVANGELISM

To be strategic in gathering the harvest, it is important to seek God for direction on where to cast the spiritual net.

> *John 21:6, "And He said unto them, Cast the net on the right side of the ship, and ye shall find. They cast therefore, and now they were not able to draw it for the multitude of fishes."*

When the disciples cast the net where Jesus directed, they received a multitude of fish. Even as we seek the Lord for where to cast the net, we should expect to reap a harvest as we follow through on the Lord's directive.

HEARING THE VOICE OF GOD

God still speaks to His people, even as He spoke to His people in the days of the first century church, and desires that we know His voice and hear Him clearly. He speaks in that still small voice that we become more familiar with as we faithfully seek Him in times of quiet devotion.

> *Acts 8:26, "And the angel of the Lord spake unto Philip, saying, Arise, and go toward the south unto the way that goeth down from Jerusalem unto Gaza, which is desert."*

Just as the angel of the Lord spoke and led Phillip to the desert to encounter the Ethiopian eunuch so the eunuch would receive the word of God and be saved, God desires to also direct His people. Whether we go out to minister as a team or encounter individuals as we go about our everyday lives, God seeks to speak to us and use us to minister to others. Let us pray for divine encounters that lead to divine impact.

PRAYER EXPECTATION IN EVANGELISM

> *Jeremiah 1:11-12, "God's Message came to me: 'What do you see, Jeremiah?' I said, 'A walking stick - that's all.' And God said, 'Good eyes! I'm*

> *sticking with you. I'll make every word I give you come true.'" (The Message Bible)*

When we pray as led by the Spirit of God we should expect God to honor our prayers and perform His word. God is moved by our faith and calls for us to pray in faith.

As we minister we should expect God to show up supernaturally and bring about divine encounters. The word of God says the people of God would do the greater works.

> *John 14:12, "Verily, verily, I say unto you, he that believeth on Me, the works that I do shall he do also; and greater works than these shall he do; because I go unto my Father."*

We should expect God to give us opportunities to share the gospel as a result of our intercession and prepare ourselves in the word of God for these encounters.

> *I Peter 3:15, "But sanctify the Lord God in your hearts: and be ready always to give an answer to every man that asketh you a reason of the hope that is in you with meekness and fear."*

We should expect our ministry efforts to be fruitful and have lasting impact as we align ourselves with God's will and purposes.

> *John 15:16, "Ye have not chosen me, but I have chosen you, and ordained you, that ye should go and bring forth fruit, and that your fruit should remain: that whatsoever ye shall ask of the Father in my name, He may give it you."*

We should expect to see multiplication of disciples as we are faithful to our prayer assignment, gather the harvest strategically, and align ourselves with a first century model of evangelism.

> *Acts 6:7, "And the word of God increased; and the number of the disciples multiplied in Jerusalem greatly; and a great company of the priests were obedient to the faith."*

PRAYER - DISCIPLESHIP - REPRODUCTION

It is important that new believers are covered in prayer following a decision for Christ. The seed of the word that has been planted within their hearts is watered through prayer.

It is important that prayers are made for new believers so that the initial "decision" for Christ leads to submission to God and to "discipleship." The church is called to make disciples not decisions only.

It is important that prayers are made for the new disciple as they journey through the process of growth and maturity.

PRAYER RESULTS:
KINGDOM MULTIPLICATION AND DOMINION
Visible and Invisible Change

The results of consistent, sustained, strategic and faith filled prayers coupled with evangelism will lead to tangible results. The invisible change realized through prayer over the course of time leads to visible change that can be measured in the natural. There will be changes in the spiritual climate that affect activities in the earthly realm. Visible change may be measured in crime rates, in areas of economics, government, education or other areas.

GOD SAVES INDIVIDUALS AND WHOLE HOUSEHOLDS

Acts 16:15, "And when she was baptized, and her household, she besought us, saying, If ye have judged me to be faithful to the Lord, come into my house, and abide there. And she constrained us."

God desires that individuals are reconciled to Him but He is also mindful of the entire household. As we minister evangelistically, we should also be mindful of the individual and their household. When individuals and whole households give their lives to Christ in great numbers, an increase of disciples is seen in that region which in turn brings a greater Kingdom influence.

CONCLUSION

As it has been emphasized throughout this chapter, prayer is so vital to the fruitfulness of evangelistic efforts. In the place of prayer and intercession we partner with the Holy Spirit and align our hearts with God's desires. In order for prayer to be most effective, the prayers must be faith filled, strategic and consistent. Prayer in evangelism should not be looked upon as a necessary exercise in ministry and given a low level of importance, but should be given its proper place in ministry. As more and more individuals and churches are committed to strategic prayer coupled with evangelism the results will be a change in the spiritual climate of territories and multiplication of disciples. If the church truly desires to see Kingdom expansion, a commitment to the ministry of prayer and evangelism is necessary.

REFLECTION

1. According to the content of this chapter, what is the definition of "Strategic Prayer and Evangelism"?

2. What are some of the barriers to intimacy with God?

3. Have you experienced barriers to intimacy with God that have not been outlined in this lesson? If so, what has been done to overcome those barriers?

4. What is the purpose of prayer walking?

5. What might cause prayer and evangelism efforts to be unfruitful and how can this be overcome?

•

REFERENCE

1. *"Evangelism That Works," George Barna, 1995, page 128*
2. *Darrel Davis, Foundation Ministries,* http://www.onlyfoundation.org, *Community Evangelism Seminar*
3. *Ibid*

4. *Ibid*
5. *Merriam-Webster Online* http://www.merriam-webster.com
6. *Free Online Dictionary* http://www.thefreedictionary.com
7. *Darrel Davis, Foundation Ministries,* http://www.onlyfoundation.org, *Community Evangelism Seminar*
8. *Ibid*
9. *Ibid*

-Nine-
EVANGELISTIC STRATEGIES FOR KINGDOM HARVEST

FOUNDATION

The heart of our God for the harvest was revealed more than two thousand years ago when He sent His Son into the earth to suffer and die for the sins of the entire world (John 1:29; I John 2:2). Without the shed blood of Jesus Christ, He being our atonement for sin and the perfect sacrifice, there would be no cleansing of sin (Hebrews 9:11-28). God so loved the world that He provided a way for man to be forgiven and enter into His Kingdom. An incredible sacrifice was paid for the harvest as Jesus suffered for the love of mankind in obedience to the Father. Even today, God "so loves the world", as He is the same God yesterday, today, and forever, and desires to see multitudes of souls come to repentance, enter into His Kingdom and come into relationship with Him.

After the resurrection of Jesus, and prior to the ascension of our Lord, the apostles received a mandate to make disciples of all nations. The work of gathering the harvest was given to the apostles to be carried out through the church.

> *Matthew 28:19, "Go therefore and make disciples of all the nations, baptizing them in the name of the Father and of the Son and of the Holy Spirit." (New King James Version)*

The work of gathering the harvest through the preaching and teaching of the gospel, and making disciples, was a priority for the first century church as is evident from the book of Acts. Multitudes of souls were added to the church (Acts 5:14, Acts 6:1, Acts 6:7).

While revival has been taking place in certain parts of the world, and more and more are becoming disciples in places such as China, regions of South America and even the Middle East, there are other parts of the world that are not seeing multitudes of souls being added to the church. Places such as Europe and the United States, where church numbers appear to be stagnant according to recent statistics, are not experiencing such revival. Unfortunately in many or most churches in the United States, making disciples has not been a priority; even though many churches will express that missions and outreach is important.

In order for multitudes of disciples to be added to the church today, God's people must be willing to evangelize and the heart of the church must be enlarged with the love and the compassion of God for souls. God has called His people to open their eyes to see the harvest and desires to equip and direct His people in the gathering of the harvest. As we, the church, posture ourselves in seeking the Lord through prayer on *HOW* to gather the harvest, God will release His wisdom, vision and strategies. In order for the church to be effective in gathering the harvest and making disciples, there must be intentional utilization of spirit directed strategies.

STRATEGIES FOR THE HARVEST - PREPARATION
Luke 14:28-33, "For which of you, intending to build a tower, sitteth not down first, and counteth the cost, whether he have sufficient to finish it? Lest

haply, after he hath laid the foundation, and is not able to finish it, all that behold it begin to mock him, Saying, This man began to build, and was not able to finish. Or what king, going to make war against another king, sitteth not down first, and consulteth whether he be able with ten thousand to meet him that cometh against him with twenty thousand? Or else, while the other is yet a great way off, he sendeth an ambassage, and desireth conditions of peace. So likewise, whosoever he be of you that forsaketh not all that he hath, he cannot be my disciple."

In the preceding scripture reference, the people were challenged to count up the cost of becoming a disciple of Jesus Christ. Even as men are challenged by the eternal words of Jesus to count up the cost of being a disciple of Jesus Christ, the church at large, and specifically the local church, must count the cost of what it will take to be a people that are used to gather a fruitful harvest. Preparation for gathering the harvest should include an assessment of what is required or what the costs will be in order for the ministry effort to be fruitful.

The apostolic mandate of going into "all the world to preach the gospel" is a command and not an option for the church. How will the harvest be gathered? What will be the tools? What resources are needed? How do we prepare ourselves to be most effective? How do we overcome the obstacles of apathy, lack of passion, fear and other challenges that are a hindrance to the work of evangelism? All of these questions need to be answered, but the answers will not come from the carnal mind of man. The answers won't come through "good idea" initiatives that can at times produce a momentary excitement and interest in evangelism, but the answer will come as God's people seek the Lord sincerely and posture their hearts humbly. In the place of seeking, the Lord God reveals His heart, His vision, His wisdom, His plans and overall strategies for gathering the harvest. God equips His people for that which He calls them to do.

PREPARATION OF THE HEART
Isaiah 6:8, "Then I heard the Lord asking, 'Whom should I send as a messenger to this people? Who will go for us?' I said, 'Here I am. Send me.'" (New Living Translation)

In the heavenly encounter that the Prophet Isaiah described in the sixth chapter of the book of Isaiah, he saw the Lord in His majesty and His holiness. Isaiah must have felt so unworthy, so naked and uncovered, and so overcome by the reverential fear of God that the scripture reads, "Then said I, Woe is me! for I am undone; because I am a man of unclean lips, and I dwell in the midst of a people of unclean lips: for mine eyes have seen the King, the LORD of hosts" (Isaiah 6:5). God knowing the heart and thoughts of Isaiah cleansed him. Isaiah 6:6-7 says, "Then flew one of the seraphims unto me, having a live coal in his hand, which he had taken with the tongs from off the altar: And he laid it upon my mouth, and said, Lo, this hath touched thy lips; and thine iniquity is taken away, and thy sin purged."

Isaiah was able to respond to the Lord with a heart of willingness, knowing he had just been cleansed by the Lord, when he heard the words, "Who will go for us?" Isaiah responded by saying, "send me." It was from a place of beholding the majesty, beauty and holiness of the Lord, and being cleansed by Him that Isaiah responded to God with a willing heart.

The church must come into new levels of prayer and intimacy in order for the heart to be prepared "to go" and to move with God in the work of evangelism. Although the Great Commission is a great mandate, evangelism should be done from a place of love for the Lord, and compassion for the lost, and not simply out of obligation. Love and compassion for the lost are birthed and cultivated in the place of prayer and worship.

PREPARATION IN THE WORD AND RIGHTEOUSNESS

I Peter 3:15-16, "But sanctify the Lord God in your hearts: and be ready always to give an answer to every man that asketh you a reason of the hope that is in you with meekness and fear: Having a good conscience; that, whereas they speak evil of you, as of evildoers, they may be ashamed that falsely accuse your good conversation in Christ."

The preceding scripture tells us that we need to always "be ready to give an answer to every man" that wants to know of the hope we have in Christ Jesus and to give that answer in a spirit of meekness.

As believers, we must study the word of God and prepare ourselves to communicate with people having a good biblical foundation. Some believers say that they don't like to share their faith because they feel unprepared or have a need for more teaching. Yet some of the same people who express this may not be willing to change their ways and begin to study and prepare. While a new believer with a few verses and a testimony can be a witness for Jesus, we must prepare ourselves to share with unbelievers of various backgrounds whether they are atheist, agnostic, embracing false religions, foreigners, or whomever.

> *Romans 2:21-24, "Thou therefore which teachest another, teachest thou not thyself? thou that preachest a man should not steal, dost thou steal? Thou that sayest a man should not commit adultery, dost thou commit adultery? thou that abhorrest idols, dost thou commit sacrilege? Thou that makest thy boast of the law, through breaking the law dishonourest thou God? For the name of God is blasphemed among the Gentiles through you, as it is written."*

The preceding scripture references the hypocrisy of the Pharisees and religious Jews that preach the law but don't live the law. The Jews were warned that they will not escape God's judgment in that they judge another man's unrighteousness while yet being unrighteous themselves.

Even today the minister of the gospel, those that witness of Jesus and share His word, cannot be given to an unholy lifestyle. Believers that proclaim the word of God must live the word of God. When we as believers preach a message of deliverance from sin, the hearer of that message should see some evidence in our lives that we have experienced deliverance from the bondage of sin and have a testimony.

In I Peter 3:16, we are told we should have a good conscience when giving an answer to unbelievers of our hope and trust in Jesus Christ. The scripture goes on to explain that if the unbeliever falsely accuses the believer, they should be ashamed of bringing an accusation after seeing our good conversation (lifestyle).

Preparation for Kingdom harvest involves both study and living a lifestyle of holiness (Hebrews 12:14).

PREPARATION IN THE SPIRIT

> *Luke 4:18-19, "The Spirit of the Lord is upon me, because He hath anointed me to preach the gospel to the poor; He hath sent me to heal the brokenhearted, to preach deliverance to the captives, and recovering of sight to the blind, to set at liberty them that are bruised, To preach the acceptable year of the Lord."*

It is God that equips His people to preach the gospel and make disciples of all nations. He anoints believers to preach the gospel to those who are both spiritually and naturally poor. He anoints believers to heal the brokenhearted, to minister healing from sickness and disease, and to preach deliverance to those who have been held captive by the devil and blinded from the truth.

> *Acts 1:8, "But ye shall receive power, after that the Holy Ghost is come upon you: and ye shall be witnesses unto me both in Jerusalem, and in all Judaea, and in Samaria, and unto the uttermost part of the earth."*

Following the ascension of Jesus, the apostles were commanded to wait for the promise of the Father which we know from scripture was the promise of the Holy Spirit baptism (Acts 2:1-4). We see in Acts 1:8 that Jesus said to them that they would receive power and then be witnesses in every territory unto the end of the earth. The receiving of the promise and the power by the Holy Spirit was ordained of God to precede their mission to be a witness for Him.

The church will not be effective in gathering the harvest without the power of the Holy Spirit, the leading and governing of the Holy Spirit, the teaching of the Holy Spirit, the strategies of the Holy Spirit and all that the Holy

Spirit provides. While we must seek to know the word of God which we preach, we also need the power of the Holy Spirit behind those words to accomplish what God desires.

> *I Corinthians 2:4-5, "And my speech and my preaching was not with enticing words of man's wisdom, but in demonstration of the Spirit and of power: That your faith should not stand in the wisdom of men, but in the power of God."*

PREPARATION IN VISION

> *John 4:35, "Say not ye, There are yet four months, and then cometh harvest? behold, I say unto you, Lift up your eyes, and look on the fields; for they are white already to harvest."*

Jesus told the disciples "lift up your eyes." He wanted them to see what He could see. Jesus saw a field that was white and ready for harvest. Without a heavenly perspective or God given vision, the disciples would have missed what the Lord was saying and been unable to visualize a ripe harvest.

There are many today that don't evangelize because they don't see a ready harvest and don't see how they could be effective at gathering a harvest. God desires to give spiritual vision to His sons and daughters and bring about an alignment with His vision. God wants His church to see what He sees. God wants His people to see through the eyes of faith and see the gathering of harvest in the spirit realm before it is fully realized in the natural realm.

In the place of prayer and the place of meditation upon the word of God, He causes our faith to be strengthened and our vision to receive clarity so that we can be like Caleb, who knew that the obstacles he saw in Canaan could be overcome, even with giants occupying in the land (Numbers 13:25-33).

> *Numbers 13:30, "And Caleb stilled the people before Moses, and said, Let us go up at once, and possess it; for we are well able to overcome it."*

Although Caleb saw the land of Canaan being occupied by a great and strong people just as the other eleven with him, Caleb must have been able to visualize Israel occupying the land before the land was ever conquered and occupied by the Jews. Caleb received a God given perspective and was able to see through the eyes of faith and trust in the promises of God in spite of the perceived obstacles.

The church must have a God given vision for the harvest in order to be consistent and effective at gathering the harvest.

PREPARATION -
UNDERSTANDING YOUR HARVEST TYPE

> *I Corinthians 9:19-23, "Even though I am a free man with no master, I have become a slave to all people to bring many to Christ. When I was with the Jews, I lived like a Jew to bring the Jews to Christ. When I was with those who follow the Jewish law, I too lived under that law. Even though I am not subject to the law, I did this so I could bring to Christ those who are under the law. When I am with the Gentiles who do not follow the Jewish law, I too live apart from that law so I can bring them to Christ. But I do not ignore the law of God; I obey the law of Christ. When I am with those who are weak, I share their weakness, for I want to bring the weak to Christ. Yes, I try to find common ground with everyone, doing everything I can to save some. I do*

everything to spread the Good News and share in its blessings." (New Living Translation)

In the above referenced scripture the apostle Paul explained that he purposed to find common ground with everyone in order to share the gospel with them. It is important to come to understand the culture of the people we aim to reach and learn how to be most effective in communicating with them. This involves not only preparation in the word of God but preparation in studying and researching the cultural background of a group of people or a certain demographic. The church at times has been guilty of trying to communicate the message of the gospel without investing time to understand the cultural background of a group of people in order to be most effective or even culturally sensitive.

There may be numerous times believers may unexpectedly encounter people of different cultural backgrounds. They may desire to minister to them while having little to no understanding of their background. We cannot *pre*-pare for every instance and must trust in the Holy Spirit when God brings about these divine encounters. Yet in order to be most effective in evangelistic ministry when targeting a certain group of people with the gospel message, preparation in cultural study, demographics and needs assessment is needed and is wise.

PREPARATION TO OVERCOME
1 John 4:4, "Ye are of God, little children, and have overcome them: because greater is He that is in you, than he that is in the world."

When God commanded the apostles to go and make disciples of all nations, the early church did not carry out this mandate without encountering opposition. Yet God worked through them in such a way that even the unbelieving Jews, in their opposition and anger, referred to the apostles as those who have "turned the world upside down" (Acts 17:5-7). So then, in spite of the opposition, encountering those who refused to believe, having their lives threatened, being jailed, and experiencing even physical discomforts for the sake of the gospel, the word of God prevailed and the number of disciples multiplied (Acts 6:7).

The apostles were not able to prevail against opposition in their own strength but by and through the Spirit of God that dwelled within them. The "Greater One" within them enabled them to overcome the opposition in the world, both that which was observed in the natural realm and the opposition unseen in the spirit realm. God took ordinary people and put His Spirit in them causing them to do extraordinary things and overcome great obstacles.

> *II Corinthians 1:8-10, "For we would not, brethren, have you ignorant of our trouble which came to us in Asia, that we were pressed out of measure, above strength, insomuch that we despaired even of life: But we had the sentence of death in ourselves, that we should not trust in ourselves, but in God which raiseth the dead: Who delivered us from so great a death, and doth deliver: in whom we trust that he will yet deliver us."*

It is important that we be reminded that the apostles had to deal with their own humanity in being obedient to the call of making disciples, for at times they were pressed out of measure, above strength, and even despaired of life according to scripture. The apostles had great victories but they also must have surely had times where they had to press past obstacles of fear, doubt, weariness, lack of resources, support, or lack of expectation and vision. Yet in spite of these things, they chose not to trust in themselves but in God who raises the dead.

In order to overcome and experience the fruit of our evangelistic efforts, the church must be willing to overcome:
- the natural and spiritual opposition,
- apathy and receive the compassion of God,
- fear and move in spiritual boldness,
- ignorance and receive revelation and understanding,
- limited prayer and move in consistent prayer,
- limited vision and receive prophetic vision,
- limited faith, and move with unlimited faith.

By the power of the Holy Spirit, the church will prevail.

STRATEGIES FOR THE HARVEST - PLAN AND IMPLEMENTATION

Proverbs 3:6, "In all thy ways acknowledge Him, and He shall direct thy paths."

Obtaining a plan or strategy for winning the lost and making disciples starts with acknowledging the Lord first. This might seem simplistic and something that every mature Christian should know, yet there have been many church initiatives that have been "good ideas" yet were not birthed from a place of seeking the Lord for His strategies and plans for implementation.

Unfortunately, the ministry of prayer has often not been the most vibrant and strongly supported ministry of the church in many local churches. Many believers even acknowledge having much less time in prayer then they believe they should. When there is not a strong prayer culture within the local church it provides for a greater opportunity to develop plans and produce initiatives that are not born from the heart and mind of God. This therefore hinders the spiritual momentum of the church as well as causes the church to use time and resources inappropriately. The lack of strong consistent prayer causes the church to not focus on God's priorities in a particular season. Then the assumption can be made that the "good idea" initiatives are God's priorities.

When praying and seeking the Lord for strategies to gather and disciple the harvest, as well as plans for implementation, we are trusting God to… (1) Identify our harvest fields or territories, (2) Reveal which evangelistic methods will be most effective in gathering the harvest, (3) Identify the demonic hindrances to gathering the harvest and receive a strategy to confront the spiritual opposition, (4) Identify what resources (money, finances, facilities, etc.) are needed to gather the harvest, (5) Provide a plan for mobilization of believers for evangelistic ministry, (6) Provide a plan for establishing evangelism as a part of the culture of the church and lifestyle of the believer, (7) Provide the labourers as we pray to the "Lord of the Harvest," (8) Provide a plan for how to prepare the church for receiving and discipling new believers, (9) Provide the resources to help nurture both the spiritual and natural development of the new believers, (10) Provide a plan for developing relationships within the secular community and open opportunities to partner for community transformation while gaining recognition as a relevant voice in the community.

Exodus 35:30-33, "And Moses said unto the children of Israel, See, the LORD hath called by name Bezaleel the son of Uri, the son of Hur, of the tribe

> *of Judah; And he hath filled him with the spirit of God, in wisdom, in understanding, and in knowledge, and in all manner of workmanship; And to devise curious works, to work in gold, and in silver, and in brass, And in the cutting of stones, to set them, and in carving of wood, to make any manner of cunning work."*

Moses was instructed to build the tabernacle and in order to do the work, resources and skill coupled with wisdom was required. God instructed them to take an offering to gather the resources for the building of the tabernacle. The Lord provided laborers who were "filled with the spirit of God, in wisdom, understanding, knowledge, and in all manner of workmanship." Moses had been given the dimensions and descriptions for the tabernacle, but it was the wisdom of God and His spirit that caused that which was on His mind and heart to be manifested in the natural.

In implementing the strategies of God for gathering and discipling the harvest, it is important to tap into God's wisdom. Just as according to the book of Exodus, God gave Moses instructions and the craftsmen wisdom, knowledge and understanding in how to create items needed for the tabernacle, God will cause His church to know how to implement the strategies and plans received from heaven by His wisdom.

> *James 1:5, "If any of you lack wisdom, let him ask of God, that giveth to all men liberally, and upbraideth not; and it shall be given him."*

STRATEGIES FOR THE HARVEST - THE GATHERING

It is important that believers allow God to show us...

(1) those who are ripe for the harvest, (2) those who are still in the process of ripening, and (3) those who don't even appear to ever be a candidate for harvest (by the natural eye) yet need to have the word planted within them. As we cast the spiritual net to gather the harvest, we must trust the Holy Spirit to show us the need of each individual that we may encounter and show us where to cast the net.

> *John 21:6, "And He said unto them, Cast the net on the right side of the ship, and ye shall find. They cast therefore, and now they were not able to draw it for the multitude of fishes."*

Too often believers have pushed to get a decision for Christ when the individual was just not ready or not yet ripe for harvest. This produces an initial excitement on the part of the soul-winner about getting the decision for Christ. Yet this is often followed by the disappointment of realizing the individual was not yet ready to surrender their lives to Jesus.

> *I Corinthians 3:6, "I have planted, Apollos watered; but God gave the increase."*

Whether we are planting the word of God in a person's life or watering that which has been planted, we are being used by God as a part of His overall plan for harvest. It is God that brings the increase and uses His church as spiritual sickles in His hand for the gathering.

STRATEGIES FOR THE HARVEST - FROM DECISION TO DISCIPLE

It is important that a person goes from making a decision to follow Christ to being a willing disciple of Jesus Christ. As new believers are gathered into the church it is important to see "fruit that remains." Ultimately the desired spiritual fruit of ministry is to see new believers make a lifetime decision to submit to Jesus as their Lord and Savior. In order to transition from that initial place of "decision" to becoming a "disciple", the new believer needs to have the word of God explained to them. Jesus told the apostles to "Teach these new disciples to obey all the commands I have given you..." (Matthew 28:20a, New Living Translation).

Not many Christians refer to themselves as disciples today, but being a true Christian means being a disciple. To be a disciple, an individual must be willing to be a follower of Jesus and obedient to His teachings. There is much the Bible tells us about what is required to be a disciple.

Jesus said....

- If any man will come after me, let him deny himself, take up his cross, and follow Me (Mark 8:34).
- He that loves father or mother, son or daughter, more than Me is not worthy of Me (Matthew 10:37).
- If you continue in my word you are my disciples indeed (John 8:31).

As new believers transition from the initial decision to disciple, it is important that they come to learn and understand the word of God and become rooted and grounded in the love of God.

It is important that new believers learn and embrace a gospel that produces authentic Christianity. New believers should be engrafted into the church community. The church community must develop a culture of discipleship and mature individuals within the church must be willing to be one that disciple and nurture spiritual babies into mature believers.

STRATEGIES FOR THE HARVEST - DISCIPLES MAKING DISCIPLES

> *II Timothy 2:2, "And the things that thou hast heard of me among many witnesses, the same commit thou to faithful men, who shall be able to teach others also."*

The church should have a heavenly vision of God's plan and purpose for discipleship. God's desire is that new disciples learn and mature so that they in turn can become one who disciples others. As this process takes place and continues, Kingdom multiplication is seen as more and more people are translated from the dark kingdom of satan into the Kingdom of God.

> *Genesis 1:28, "And God blessed them, and God said unto them, Be fruitful, and multiply, and replenish the earth, and subdue it: and have dominion over the fish of the sea, and over the fowl of the air, and over every living thing that moveth upon the earth."*

STRATEGIES FOR THE HARVEST - FROM GENERATION TO GENERATION

God made a covenant with our father of faith Abraham (Romans 4:1,11). God called Abraham to not only be blessed but to "be a blessing" even to the nations. God made promises to Abraham, the father of faith, and those promises were not only to him but to the generations to come.

The church, both present and future, the spiritual descendants of Abraham, are called to be a blessing to the nations.

Genesis 22:18, "And in thy seed shall all the nations of the earth be blessed; because thou hast obeyed my voice."

Genesis 17:7, "And I will establish My covenant between Me and thee and thy seed after thee in their generations for an everlasting covenant, to be a God unto thee, and to thy seed after thee."

Romans 4:11-16, "And he received the sign of circumcision, a seal of the righteousness of the faith which he had yet being uncircumcised: that he might be the father of all them that believe, though they be not circumcised; that righteousness might be imputed unto them also: And the father of circumcision to them who are not of the circumcision only, but who also walk in the steps of that faith of our father Abraham, which he had being yet uncircumcised. For the promise, that he should be the heir of the world, was not to Abraham, or to his seed, through the law, but through the righteousness of faith. For if they which are of the law be heirs, faith is made void, and the promise made of none effect: Because the law worketh wrath: for where no law is, there is no transgression. Therefore it is of faith, that it might be by grace; to the end the promise might be sure to all the seed; not to that only which is of the law, but to that also which is of the faith of Abraham; who is the father of us all,"

It is very important that the youth within the church not only have a biblical foundation and world view, but that they understand their spiritual heritage in a biblical sense. It is important that they are trained and understand that they also are called to be a blessing in the earth, whether locally or abroad, and can be a blessing to others even now by the power of the Holy Spirit.

The youth of the church, as well as adults, need to be mobilized in evangelism so that they can reach their generation and be used of God to reap the harvest. The youth can carry a message into places not so easily accessible to the average adult such as the school systems, youth centers and other places where youth gather. The youth have a voice and can reach their peers. Strategies in evangelism should include plans to involve the youth and train them for carrying the gospel further than the generation before them.

CONCLUSION

God would not give the church the mandate to preach the gospel and make disciples of all nations without providing the desire, anointing, resources, plans and strategies to perform this task. Those who may have been faithful in evangelism but have not yet seen the desired results should remain faithful and continue to seek God concerning any obstacles to be overcome or new strategies. Strategies in evangelism that were given many years ago may not be the most effective strategy to be used today. God is always speaking and He continues to give His people new vision, perspective, anointing and new strategies when we seek Him. As God's people consistently posture themselves humbly in the place of prayer with a heart of faith and expectancy, God imparts into His people and provides what is needed to gather the harvest. As we look at the decreasing numbers in overall church attendance in the United States and the apathy among believers concerning evangelism, there is much work to be done. Those that are faithful and consistent in carrying out God's directives and strategies will see results over the course of time. Consistent prayer must cover the ministry efforts and discipleship of new believers will help them become mature believers who will be able to teach others.

May God in His mercy cause a great awakening among His people that cause believers to repent of apathy concerning souls, seek the Lord like never before and align with the Father's heart for the harvest. Amen.

REFLECTION

1. Why is spiritual vision important in evangelism ministry?

2. Why is understanding cultures important in preparing to evangelize to certain groups of people within the community?

3. What is the difference between a "good idea" and a "God idea" as it pertains to evangelistic strategy?

4. Are the youth at your church involved in evangelistic efforts? If not, what may be the reason for their lack of involvement and what changes may be needed to get them involved?

5. Some evangelistic strategies utilized in the 1980's or 90's may not be as effective today. What might be some reasons for this lack of effectiveness and what should be done?

CULMINATION

Jesus said in Matthew 16:18, "...thou art Peter, and upon this rock I will build my church; and the gates of hell shall not prevail against it." God has declared that the powers of hell will not prevail and overcome His church yet God has ordained His church to prevail over the enemy and to advance, increase and exercise dominion in the earth.

> *Luke 10:19, "Behold, I give unto you power to tread on serpents and scorpions, and over all the power of the enemy: and nothing shall by any means hurt you."*
>
> *I John 4:4, "Ye are of God, little children, and have overcome them: because greater is He that is in you, than He that is in the world."*

Increase and expansion of the church in the earth comes by many avenues. A principle avenue outlined in the scope of this book is evangelism coupled with strategic prayer and multiplication of disciples.

God has given His church spiritual keys to be utilized to accomplish His will in the earth. Spiritual keys such as faith, prayer, fasting, evangelism, healing, discipleship, worship, deliverance, spiritual gifts and many others are among them. Even in a time of rapid change in culture, religious attitudes, education and technology these spiritual keys remain powerful and the strategies of heaven given by the Holy Spirit are unlimited.

What will our urban cities look like in just a few decades? What about the church? Will we see multiplication of disciples, thriving churches and a people governing the spiritual climate of their region through prayers and intercession? The answer to these questions lie within us, the individuals that make up God's church in the earth.

There have been many books written on the subject of evangelism, prayer, discipleship, healing and other topics related to church life and ministry. There have been many book, audio and video resources made available to the church over the years that are current and easily obtained, particularly here in the United States. The challenge that we all have when completing a book designed to provide training is to ACT on what we have read and learned. My prayer is that everyone that reads this book will be challenged and inspired by the Holy Spirit to ACT and do great works for God, not out of obligation, legalism or fear but out of love and compassion.

There are multitudes upon multitudes of people in the earth waiting and looking for a true message of hope, deliverance, freedom and salvation and many are groping in the darkness trying to find their way. God has given us, His church, the way and the message. Let us commit ourselves to be one of many that will show them the way to Jesus Christ.

> *Matthew 5:13-16, "Ye are the salt of the earth: but if the salt have lost his savour, wherewith shall it be salted? it is thenceforth good for nothing, but to be*

cast out, and to be trodden under foot of men. Ye are the light of the world. A city that is set on an hill cannot be hid. Neither do men light a candle, and put it under a bushel, but on a candlestick; and it giveth light unto all that are in the house. Let your light so shine before men, that they may see your good works, and glorify your Father which is in heaven."

The scripture tell us that we are the salt of the earth and the light of the world. Let us continually be salt and light in the earth. Through prayer coupled with faith and action we should expect to see multitudes of others come into the light of God's Kingdom.

CPSIA information can be obtained
at www.ICGtesting.com
Printed in the USA
LVOW01s0813230516
489511LV00026B/616/P